Jobs,
Technology
and People

- Nik Chmiel

ROUTLEDGE

LONDON AND NEW YORK

ROUTLEDGE

First published 1998
by Routledge
11 New Fetter Lane, London
EC4P 4EE

Simultaneously published in
the USA and Canada
by Routledge
29 West 35th Street, New York
NY 10001

© 1998 Nik Chmiel

Typeset in Sabon and Futura by
Florencetype Ltd, Stoodleigh, Devon

Printed and bound in Great Britain by
TJ International Ltd, Padstow,
Cornwall

*British Library Cataloguing in
Publication Data*
A catalogue record for this book is
available from the British Library

*Library of Congress Cataloging in
Publication Data*
Chmiel, Nik.
    Jobs, technology and people /
    Nik Chmiel.
    Includes bibliographical references
    and index.
    1. Employees—Effect of
    technological innovations on.
    I. Title.
HD6331.C457   1998
658.5′14—dc21   97–50042
                                    CIP

ISBN 0–415–15816–8 (hbk)
ISBN 0–415–15817–6 (pbk)

To Kim Roman Seymour Arthur-Chmiel, born when I began writing this book, and my delight

The Master said, 'It is enough that the language one uses gets the point across.'

Confucius, *The Analects*, XV:41

Contents

Series preface ix

1 Technology and work psychology 1

2 Jobs and tasks 15

3 Technology and personnel 39

4 Mental work 65

5 Work safety in complex technological systems 91

6 Team-working and technology 113

7 Concluding remarks 133

Glossary 139
Annotated further reading 143
References 145
Index 159

Series preface

The Psychology Focus series provides short, up-to-date accounts of key areas in psychology without assuming the reader's prior knowledge in the subject. Psychology is often a favoured subject area for study, since it is relevant to a wide range of disciplines such as Sociology, Education, Nursing and Business Studies. These relatively inexpensive but focused short texts combine sufficient detail for psychology specialists with sufficient clarity for non-specialists.

The series authors are academics experienced in undergraduate teaching as well as research. Each takes a key topic within their area of psychological expertise and presents a short review, highlighting important themes and including both theory and research findings. Each aspect of the topic is clearly explained with supporting glossaries to elucidate technical terms.

The series has been conceived within the context of the increasing modularisation which has been developed in higher education over the last decade and fulfils the consequent need for clear, focused, topic-based course material. Instead of following one course of study, students on a modularisation programme are often able to choose modules from a wide range of disciplines to complement the modules they are required to study for a specific degree. It can no longer be assumed that students studying a particular module will necessarily have the same background knowledge (or lack of it!) in that subject. But they will need to familiarise themselves with a particular topic rapidly since a single module in a single topic may be only fifteen weeks long with assessments arising during that period. They may have to combine eight or more modules in a single year to obtain a degree at the end of their programme of study.

One possible problem with studying a range of separate modules is that the relevance of a particular topic or the relationship between topics may not always be apparent. In the Psychology Focus series authors, where possible, have drawn on practical and applied examples to support the points being made so that readers can see the wider relevance of the topic under study. Also, the study of psychology is usually broken up into separate areas, such as social psychology, developmental psychology or cognitive psychology, to take three examples. Whilst the books in the Psychology Focus series will provide excellent coverage of certain key topics within these 'traditional' areas, the authors have not been constrained in their examples and explanations and may draw on material across the whole field of psychology to help explain the topic under study more fully.

Each text in the series provides the reader with a range of important material on a specific topic. They are suitably comprehensive and give a clear account of the important issues involved. The authors analyse and interpret the material as well as present an up-to-date and detailed review of key work. Recent references are provided along with suggested further reading to allow readers to investigate the topic in more depth. It is hoped, therefore, that after following the informative review of a key topic in a Psychology Focus text, readers will not only have a clear understanding of the issues in question but will be intrigued and challenged to investigate the topic further.

Note: Annotated further reading for *Jobs, Technology and People* is supplied after the Glossary; see p. 143. The author felt that because his was an integrative study and additional books are topic-based it was better to provide a few books which reflected the wide variety of topics and link these to particular chapters.

Chapter 1

Technology and work psychology

■ Technology and work   3

■ Psychology and work   6
  Early perspectives   6
  Occupational psychology in the UK   8

■ Research in occupational psychology   9
  Contexts for research knowledge   12

■ Summary of the book   13

THE INDUSTRIALISED COUNTRIES are in the midst of a technological revolution, probably every bit as significant as the industrial revolution. The industrial revolution brought about dramatic changes in the way in which society and work were organised in the UK (e.g. Messinger, 1985), and now the technological revolution again promises equally radical changes to our working lives. At a global, and necessarily simplified, level, the industrial revolution brought about a change from feudal society to one ordered by work imperatives. Prior to the industrialisation of the UK, work was mostly done on a casual basis in the sense that certain periods of the year – for example, harvest time – required considerable effort, whilst other times did not demand so much. The change to an economy dominated by factory production and urbanisation necessitated constant effort in pursuit of production. Ironically, the promise of computerised technology is more flexibility in the means of production. What this may entail for people at work remains to be seen, but some commentators forecast a return to the casualisation of labour, with only those who possess the appropriate skills for the technological age able to get work. One thing is becoming clear, however, and that is that work is changing, with higher levels of knowledge and skill being required than hitherto. In manufacturing, for example, the pressure appears to be in the direction of increasing the level and range of skills of those in employment, with **automation** increasingly taking over previously manual jobs. The shift is from physical to mental labour.

This book is an introduction to several aspects of the psychology of jobs and technology. Its emphasis is on psychological analyses at the individual level. Thus, for example, attitudes, perceptions and mental capabilities form core concerns in relation to technology and work. The book is not about organisational psychology and organisational levels of analysis *per se*,

2

although these are mentioned where relevant. The book does not cover the whole field of work and organisational psychology, but rather focuses largely on what has been called 'human factors'. Furthermore, the book concentrates on topic areas and theories which are mainstream in what could be called 'fitting the person to the job and technology, and the job and technology to the person'. Thus areas covered include job and task design, selection, assessment and training, work and task demands, safety at work, and working in teams. The purpose of the book is to introduce these areas to those without previous knowledge of them, and to illustrate how relevant psychological knowledge is to the analysis of jobs and technology. Therefore dominant perspectives and findings are presented and explained. Necessarily this has resulted in some views being given less prominence than others. Readers are provided with references to more detailed texts to follow up should they wish to. Those who should find the book useful to them include students of work psychology, business studies, engineering and related disciplines, those who work with technology, for example nurses using modern medical equipment, and those whose job entails considering the impact of new technology, and who want to know more about the psychology involved.

Technology and work

The history of technology at work since the industrial revolution can be divided into three phases: power provision; automation of function; and information and control of process.

Traditional manufacturing technology most often was an aid to work, especially physical work. Thus steam was harnessed for power and used to drive weaving machinery, for example. The machines were still controlled by people. Later, machinery became sufficiently sophisticated to automate some functions performed previously by people. Later still, in the third phase, the change from traditional to computerised technologies in the last few years has involved the extensive use of computers to control technology.

The capabilities of computers lie in the capture, storage, manipulation and distribution of information, and it is these capabilities that allow for the automation and control of production and service operations. The technology can be used in at least three ways: to provide feedback to the operators of the technology; to control a process in a predetermined way; and to detect faulty equipment and initiate corrective action. In addition to the foregoing, computers can also promote organisational integration through providing information to different levels and areas, and more quickly.

McLoughlin and Clark (1994) detail a slightly different set of three phases in manufacturing automation: primary mechanisation, which was the use of water or steam power to replace human physical and manual labour in the transformation of raw materials into products; secondary mechanisation, which used electricity, and facilitated continuous-flow assembly lines and processes; and tertiary mechanisation, which used electronics-based computing and information technologies to co-ordinate and control production tasks. They report that primary mechanisation was predominant up to the end of the nineteenth century, and that since 1945 tertiary mechanisation has assumed increasing importance.

Estimates suggest that by the end of the 1980s, 52,500 computer-based systems had been installed in UK manufacturing, and that the rate of adoption of information technology grew to the extent that in 1987, establishments using **microelectronics** in production amounted to 59 per cent of the total establishments, and accounted for 82 per cent of total UK manufacturing employment. The 1990 Workplace Industrial Relations Survey (WIRS) showed that 23 per cent of all manual workplaces with over 25 employees had experienced technological change in the previous three years. For large manufacturing plants, employing over 100 employees, the figure was 55 per cent. Taking the UK as a whole, Foley et al. (1993) reported figures for 1987 showing that 31 per cent of establishments had computer-aided design (CAD) workstations, that 28 per cent had computer numeric controlled (CNC) machine tools, and 46 per cent had programmable logic controllers. By 1991, in Sheffield, well known for steel manufacture and associated industries, 57 per cent of establishments had CNC installations.

The impact of computer information and control systems has been great in manufacturing, but has not been confined to that sector of the economy. In the service sector McLoughlin and Clark (1994) point out that computer-based activities have generally been a more recent happening. Administration and financial services have also taken up computer-based technologies. Overall, the 1990 WIRS showed that 75 per cent of work establishments had some kind of on-site computing facility compared to 47 per cent in 1984, and that for workplaces with non-manual employees, 52 per cent had experienced technological change in the previous three years.

McLoughlin and Clark (1994) propose that the net effect of this change is that the nature of work has shifted from physical to mental labour. They detail two case studies, one from the communications industry and one from the engineering design sector, to support their conclusion that new technology has reduced the requirement for manual skills and dexterity, and has placed increased emphasis on mental skills and abilities in order that the new technologies are used effectively. One of the case studies involved telephone exchanges, and the change from electromechanical to electronic routeing of calls through the exchange. The new technology involved completely changing the way a caller is switched through to the called telephone number. They report that the skills required for maintenance tasks showed a qualitative change from those needed under the old system. The new technology placed a strong emphasis on mental diagnostic skills.

McLoughlin and Clark's broad conclusion is supported by other evidence. Foley *et al.* (1993), in a survey of metal-related industries in Sheffield, UK, concluded that training needs were increased considerably by the introduction of new technology. Machin (1995), in a report on the demand for skills in the UK labour market, concluded that there has been a considerable shift away from manual to non-manual labour in UK manufacturing, and towards the use of more skilled labour. McLoughlin and Clark (1994, p. 152) suggest that

JOBS, TECHNOLOGY AND PEOPLE

when a new technology is introduced into the production process the work tasks that have to be accomplished also change. However, this still leaves open important questions of whether and how these new work tasks are to be allocated to existing jobs or grouped into new ones, and how these jobs are to be linked into a more general pattern of work organisation.

Psychologists are concerned with just these issues, amongst others, and have spent most of the twentieth century studying them from a psychological perspective. The following sections are designed to provide a broad context for the rest of the book, and give a brief overview of the concerns and methods of psychology at work.

Psychology and work

The psychology of work is concerned with the feelings, attitudes, behaviour and performance of those at work. It is also preoccupied with those factors of jobs, work environment, organisational structure and management which influence workers' attitudes and behaviour.

In the UK this area of study is covered by occupational psychology. In continental Europe it is called work psychology or work and organisational psychology, and in North America it is called industrial and organisational psychology.

Early perspectives

Areas of concern in the first half of the twentieth century were how jobs should be designed and managed, working conditions and fatigue at work (which related to workload, hours of work, and the limitations in workers' capabilities), and army recruitment (which was a personnel selection issue) (see Holloway, 1991, for an extended discussion).

One of the dominant approaches to the way jobs should be viewed was the philosophy of '**scientific management**' espoused by Frederick W. Taylor, an industrial engineer at the Midvale Steel Company, Philadelphia, around the turn of the century. His views were founded on the premise that people are motivated primarily by economic factors, and hence hard work should be linked to pay. He argued that work should be standardised on the most efficient way of doing it, and 'time and motion' studies of metal cutting were carried out to establish this. Thereafter workers were paid on a piecework basis: in other words, so much pay for so much work. The approach of scientific management demanded that the knowledge and skills needed to carry out production processes became vested in management. Shopfloor workers were then told how, when, and in how much time, they should carry out tasks assigned to them. Supervisors became very important in the system.

A second major influence on how work should be seen came from studies done at the Hawthorne plant of the Western Electrical Company in Chicago, from about 1924 to 1932. The researchers demonstrated that social relations at work, and not just economic self-interest, were important for productivity. In one set of observations a small number of women workers were transferred from their usual work area to a separate test area. There the workers experienced a series of controlled changes to their conditions of work, such as hours of work, duration of rest pauses and provision of refreshments. During the changes the observer maintained a friendly manner, consulting with the workers, listening to their complaints, and keeping them informed of the experiment. Following all but one of the changes there was a continuous increase in production. The researchers formed the conclusion that the interest shown in the workers, and the additional attention given to them, was the principal reason for the higher productivity. This is known as the **Hawthorne effect**.

Another set of observations involved a group of men. It was noted that the men developed their own informal pattern of social relations and 'norms' for working behaviour. Despite a financial incentive scheme which offered more money for more productivity, the group chose a level of output well below what they were capable of producing.

7

The psychology of work has expanded dramatically in the time since the Second World War, and is now an important part of professional psychology. There is an increasing recognition of the usefulness that contemporary occupational psychology can provide in the understanding of work activity.

Occupational psychology in the UK

Since 1971 the British Psychological Society has had a Division of Occupational Psychology which has three main aims: to develop the practice of occupational psychology; to promote high standards of professional competence and behaviour amongst occupational psychologists; and to increase public awareness of occupational psychology for the advantage of individuals and organisations. The division oversees professional development and sets the standards for becoming a chartered occupational psychologist. Chartered occupational psychologists are concerned with the performance of people at work and in training, with developing an understanding of how organisations function and how individuals and groups behave at work. Their aim is to increase effectiveness, efficiency and satisfaction at work.

The main areas in which occupational psychologists have skills are: personnel selection and assessment; identification of training needs; organisational change and development; interviewing techniques; performance appraisal systems; vocational guidance and counselling; job and task design; group and inter-group processes and skills; design of and adaptation to new technology; career and management development; industrial relations; **ergonomics** and equipment design; attitude and opinion surveys; occupational safety; design and evaluation training; equal employment opportunity; and stress management.

The Division of Occupational Psychology delineates eight main areas for occupational psychology in which members of the division should demonstrate knowledge. These are:

- human–machine interaction
- design of environments and work, health and safety

- personnel selection and assessment, including test and exercise design
- performance appraisal and career development
- counselling and personal development
- training (identification of needs, training design and evaluation)
- employee relations and motivation
- organisational development.

Applicants for membership of the division will generally have in-depth experience of at least one of the four main practice areas of occupational psychology, which are: work and the work environment (including health and safety); the individual (including assessment, selection, guidance and counselling); organisational development and change; and training.

Although much of the work of occupational psychologists is practical in nature, the strength of their advice is based on knowledge acquired systematically, through scientific means where possible. Thus research into behaviour at work plays an extremely important part in informing professional practice, as well as in developing more fundamental theories into the psychology of people at work, and how this is influenced by the context of work organisations.

Research in occupational psychology

There are two traditional types of ways to gather knowledge about work: by experiment, and by the use of correlational studies, explained below. Recently other ways, such as case studies, have also become more accepted (see Robson, 1993, for a detailed discussion). Within these three main approaches a variety of information-gathering techniques and analyses can be deployed, ranging from interviews and questionnaires on the one hand, to behavioural observation on the other. Some techniques fit better within some approaches than others, though. Thus the case study approach often goes with interviews, whereas there are difficulties in using interview data in an experimental analysis.

Experiments, whether in the laboratory or the field, allow inferences to be made about causality between the variables studied, whereas correlational studies observe only whether factors change alongside others; causality cannot be inferred. Case studies provide a very rich picture of a particular work setting, but the picture may not generalise to other settings. Occupational psychologists are often limited to observing natural variation and change within organisations and work settings, and hence experimentation is difficult. Many studies tend to be correlational in nature. However, despite the constraints of the work environment some field experimentation is possible and fruitful.

Field experimentation has the same procedure as laboratory-based methods, and tries to follow them as closely as possible. Thus an experiment involves forming a hypothesis, selecting experimental and control groups, introducing an experimental manipulation, measuring the change and making inferences as to causality. However, it may not always be possible to achieve the ideal experimental constraints in the field. Thus control and experimental groups may not be randomly determined, and other factors may alter along with the experimental manipulation.

The advantage of the field experiment over a laboratory-based one is that the real-life conditions of the work setting can be preserved, in contrast to the artificial environment of the laboratory. For some investigations this is crucial; for others it is not, and the laboratory is the best place to produce the knowledge required. In addition to deliberately changing workplace factors to investigate their effect, experimenters can take advantage of naturally occurring change, especially when there is no control over the workplace, or control is undesirable. Here quasi-experimental methods are used to set up comparison groups, measure them before any change, measure them after the natural change, and analyse the results and draw causal inferences as appropriate. Often other factors also change in addition to the factor(s) of interest, and the effects of these need to be taken into account.

The experimental approach has the advantage of allowing causal inferences between variables to be drawn. However, it is often the case that such experimentation is difficult to achieve in the field, and the artificial environment of the laboratory is an impediment to finding satisfactory connections between work-related variables. Under these circumstances the correlational study comes into its own.

Correlational studies concentrate on examining what factors change together, without making any inferences as to the causal nature of the relationships. Thus manipulation and control of variables are not as important, and natural variation in the workplace is central. What matters is the degree of relationship (the correlation) between factors, and its direction; that is, whether both factors increase together (a positive correlation) or whether one factor decreases as the other increases (a nega-tive correlation). A fictitious example would be whether people who work longer hours feel less alert, but more satisfied with their work. In this case the length of the working day would correlate negatively with alertness (as the length increases, alert-ness decreases) but positively with satisfaction (as length increases, satisfaction also increases).

Finally, case studies look at individuals or small groups of people at work. Focusing on a small number of people, or a small company, provides an opportunity to look at the group in depth, and over a period of time. Case studies are most useful in an exploratory context. The case study provides for studying a situ-ation in depth, and from a variety of angles, through interviews, observations and the analysis of documentation. However, a case study does not allow statistical generalisation.

The usefulness of any of these approaches to understanding psychology at work can be greatly enhanced if the results from one work situation can be generalised to others. In order to gener-alise successfully certain conditions need to be met. The key factor is representativeness. First, if a particular finding is to generalise beyond the people involved in a study, the people studied must be representative of the larger population to which generalisations are to be made. Second, the context of a study should not constrain generalisability by findings being specific to it, or to the people studied. A fictitious example of a non-generalisable context might be work groups studied on the shop floor. A study of such groups could suggest that certain personality aspects are important to successful team-working. However, a group of office managers might work well together, but exhibit completely different personality profiles. Successful team-working attributes do not generalise across work groups in this hypothetical example.

Contexts for research knowledge

Occupational psychology is an applied discipline. Thus the issues which commonly arise are connected with how and why workers behave as they do. Companies, on the whole, want to know the answers to these questions in order to improve productivity, although they may have an interest in how satisfied their employees are. Academics, whilst possibly being concerned with productivity, are concerned to understand the fundamental aspects of human nature at work. Consultants are asked to give advice to companies and industry, usually on a case-by-case basis.

The relationship between academics, consultants and work organisations influences the type of questions, and thus the type of research that is done. Psychologists with an interest in work-related issues can adopt different roles in relation to the organisations and work culture they study. A broad division is whether the psychologist works within, and is employed by, the organisation, or whether he or she is an outsider. The psychologist could be motivated by an academic concern with theory, or by a desire to give consultancy on best practice. In most situations, though, the ability to do research or provide consultancy is heavily dependent on the co-operation of work organisations.

The kinds of psychological topics researched in the workplace are influenced to some degree by at least two large concerns: the needs of the workplace; and the person(s) giving permission for research access to the workplace.

Work organisations have purposes different from those of psychologists, although their interests may overlap. Work organisations exist to fulfil their aims and objectives. In the manufacturing industry sector these objectives could include the production of a quality product at minimum cost. In the public sector the aim could be the provision of a diversity of services within existing resources. Organisations are usually under pressure – commercial and/or political – to achieve their aims. Psychologists, on the other hand, are trying to understand people at work, and base advice on this understanding. However, psychologists research, and advise, dynamic, changing organisations subject to the pressures just outlined. It is, therefore, difficult for psychologists not to be influenced by the pressures organisations are under. Such influence can, and often does, determine the kinds of research psychologists do, and the sort of advice it is possible to give.

The person(s) giving permission to do research in the workplace is (are) often at managerial level within the work organisation. The issues management may be concerned about could differ markedly from the concerns on the 'shop floor' or lower down the organisational hierarchy. An example of the foregoing is that often it is the management who want to know the best way to select a person for a particular job, or who want to know the best way of organising work teams in order to get maximum work efficiency. Stress at work, or job dissatisfaction, may be important only in so far as it stops workers carrying out their jobs efficiently, rather than as an end in itself. Performance at work is a very prominent theme in work psychology.

Summary of the book

The first two chapters discuss two contrasting approaches to work psychology. Chapter 2 considers how jobs and work tasks are analysed and designed with the emphasis on computer-controlled technology, and then relates aspects of jobs to satisfaction with them, and stress arising from them. Chapter 3 considers how people learn mental skills and are trained, selected, motivated and appraised to meet the requirements of work. Chapter 4 considers how mental capacities relate to job and task demands, and how they change as a result of the work environment and the variations found in people. Chapter 5 then considers safety at work, particularly with reference to complex technological systems. Chapter 6 discusses team-working, in particular from the perspective of handling information and making decisions in complex work environments. Chapter 7 is a short chapter which makes some concluding observations, and links the topics discussed in the book to other areas.

Chapter 2

Jobs and tasks

■ **Computerisation and manufacturing
jobs**   16
Advanced manufacturing technology
   and work design   17

■ **Job design**   18

■ **Job redesign and performance**   22

■ **Job analysis**   24
Functional job analysis   25
Critical incidents technique   26

■ **Task analysis**   27
Hierarchical task analysis   30

■ **Job satisfaction and well-being**   31

■ **Job-related stress**   33

■ **Summary**   38

THIS CHAPTER SETS OUT to describe key approaches to the design and analysis of jobs, and to relate the design considerations and job characteristics which bear on the use of modern computer technology in industry. Jobs are usually made up of a number of different tasks. Modern manufacturing processes, controlled by computer, have raised important new issues for the design of jobs. Computer technology in the workplace brings with it the potential for considerable flexibility in the control of machinery. The tasks involved in manufacturing have altered so that, for example, much shopfloor activity is more concerned with monitoring and tending machines, rather than actively making things. The chapter draws on examples from advanced manufacturing technology in order to illustrate contemporary approaches to job design. However, the general points which emerge can be discussed and applied to other work sectors where new technology has been introduced. Thereafter the chapter discusses the effects of job characteristics on job satisfaction and job-related stress.

Computerisation and manufacturing jobs

The advent of computers able to control machinery has facilitated several changes in the way in which goods can be produced. First, computer-controlled machines and robots can carry out many manufacturing tasks using **advanced manufacturing technology** (AMT). AMT enables faster and more flexible working: machines can be reset to produce variations in basic product to meet differing customer demands through software programming. The same machinery can produce 'batches' of different product, rather than remain dedicated to precisely the same product. For example, modern mass-produced fitted kitchens come in a variety of shapes and sizes. The kitchens are assembled from flatpacks containing the parts already cut to shape. The cutting is done on computer-controlled machinery which determines how the saws and drilling and sanding equipment cut and finish the raw materials, often laminated chipboard. The production line can be producing one design at one moment, and then, once the computers are reprogrammed, another design to satisfy individual tastes in the 'look' of the kitchen. Second, raw materials can be turned into finished product using **just in time** (JIT) techniques. JIT works on the principle that a manufacturer buys in sufficient raw materials to meet customer orders, rather than holding huge stocks of raw materials and finished goods against future orders. The linking of inventory control, orders and deliveries is made easier and faster using computer technology, and saves the costs involved in storing stocks. Third, the move to 'just in time' delivery of finished product to the customer emphasises the desirability of getting the quality of the product right first time. Traditionally, quality control was a separate function which followed manufacture, and was carried out by different employees. This meant that faulty products were dealt with only at the end of the production process, leading to wasted materials and creating the need to produce more to meet orders. **Total quality management** (TQM) is an attempt to embed quality into the manufacturing process itself, by giving responsibility for quality to those making the product, by using careful product design to minimise production difficulties, and by improving production processes (Dean and Snell, 1991).

Advanced manufacturing technology and work design

The main advantage of AMT is its potential to increase throughput, enhance flexibility in response to changing market demands, improve consistency of output and reduce lead times. Dean and Snell (1991), in a survey of how new technology was implemented, concluded that it sometimes led to further simplification in shopfloor jobs, and sometimes not. In some cases operators were given increased responsibility and autonomy.

The questions raised by these observations are what job designs should be adopted with the introduction of new technology, and why?

Job design

Job design is concerned with the psychological and performance effects of general characteristics of jobs which, in principle, could be applied to any job. That is, job design is concerned with the nature of jobs and their effect on employee performance and well-being, rather than the particular content of a job. The latter is the focus of job and task analysis, discussed later in the chapter.

The term 'job design' betokens a deliberate, systematic approach to the construction of jobs and tasks. Many jobs are not 'designed' in this sense, but have evolved as a function of various factors such as economic, social and political imperatives. Examples include managerial and professional jobs. In these jobs it is more important to achieve goals than consider how those goals are achieved and the nature of the tasks involved. A key question is why have job design at all? Traditionally the answer to this question has been 'to enhance productivity'. Latterly a second consideration has been the contentment of employees. The former objective has been central to the development of jobs.

In the history of job design two clear perspectives can be discerned. The first is a systematic approach to the design of some jobs, usually 'shopfloor' jobs in industrial settings. The second is a pragmatic approach leading to research on common aspects of jobs and their relationship to psychological aspects of working life. Clearly, these two perspectives are intimately related, in that observations and principles derived from one point of view can inform the other.

In terms of modern manufacturing, at the most general level two facts are known about the effectiveness of AMT and its relationship to work design. First, most applications, though representing a major improvement on what existed before, failed to meet performance expectations (e.g. Ettlie, 1986; Jaikamur, 1986), and this is believed to be due more to work organisation than to technological factors (Office of Technology Assessment, 1984). Second, many companies have supported their systems with simplified operator job designs. Operators typically are given a restricted role in fault management. In the extreme they are required merely to load, monitor and unload the machines, and alert specialists when faults arise (Clegg and Corbett, 1986; Sepella et al., 1987; Sinclair, 1986). Therefore fault diagnosis and rectification are the province of trained experts (mechanical, electrical and electronic engineers and programmers) who do not have continuous contact with the technologies they support.

The observations about the type of preferred job design in AMT systems fits with the history of work design in the twentieth century, which shows a trend towards simplification, especially for shopfloor jobs in manufacturing (Kelly, 1982). The range of tasks within jobs and the amount of autonomy afforded to employees have been progressively reduced. A question this trend begs is why adopt this type of design?

Intellectual antecedents to **job simplification** can be found in a treatise on the political economy written by Adam Smith, a Scotsman from Kirkcaldy in Fife, and published in 1776. Smith's *Inquiry into the Nature and Causes of the Wealth of Nations* insisted on the value of the 'division of labour'. The division of labour implied that economic activity should be broken down into different component tasks, carried out by separate employees.

Around the turn of the twentieth century the philosophy of 'scientific management' was espoused by Frederick W. Taylor, an industrial engineer. As stated in Chapter 1, he argued that work should be standardised on the most efficient way of doing it, and 'time and motion' studies of metal cutting were carried out to establish what this was. 'Scientific management' embodied the division of labour in breaking down jobs into different tasks which could be carried out by different employees. In addition, the approach placed the responsibility for how, and how quickly, tasks should be done with management. Shopfloor jobs became simplified, allowing less skilled workers to carry them out with consequent savings in labour and training costs. Taylor held a strictly economic view of work motivation, and in jobs he designed workers were paid on a piecework basis: in other words, so much pay for so much work.

Taylor was able to show that his principles of 'scientific management' could produce huge increases in productivity in manual jobs. In one famous case he designed the way pig iron was handled, effecting approximately a 400 per cent increase in the amount of pig iron shifted per hour. Henry Ford instituted similar principles in creating the first **assembly line**, in order to build cars. Assembly line work is repetitive and governed by how fast the line is set up to run. Each job is concerned with only a small part of the overall product being manufactured.

Surveys have shown that 'scientific management' came to dominate western manufacturing practices in the middle of the twentieth century (e.g. Davis *et al.* 1955). There was evidence of a widespread belief that the approach of scientific management led to better productivity and cost saving. Although 'scientific management' principles originated in manufacturing industry they have been adopted wholesale in other economic sectors. For example, some fast food chains specify completely the steps from taking a customer order to the delivery of a wrapped hamburger, all within so many seconds. Different employees cover different tasks in the most efficient way possible. The operation is, literally, a fast food assembly line. Other examples include the scripting of airline ticket sales conversations. In each case jobs are simplified, and the opportunities for the worker to depart from the specified ways of doing the job are very limited.

The effect of simplified jobs on workers, however, was not positive. Such jobs were felt to be boring, tiring and not very satisfying. In addition, aspects of simplified jobs were shown to affect adversely employee well-being (Parker and Wall, 1996). Several recommendations concerning the redesign of jobs were put forward. Initially, moving workers between different tasks (job rotation), and giving workers more tasks to do in their job (job enlargement) were favoured as possible solutions.

In the 1960s, although mainly focused on motivation, views on job aspects and job satisfaction were extended by Herzberg. He proposed that two factors were involved in work motivation. 'Motivators', such as recognition, responsibility and interesting work, were considered central to feelings of job satisfaction and motivation. Other 'hygiene' factors, extrinsic to the job, such as work conditions, were felt to be important for feelings of dissatisfaction, but not crucial to motivation (see Chapter 3 for a more detailed explanation).

In a very influential analysis, Hackman and Oldham (1976) suggested that there were five aspects to jobs critical to satisfaction and performance:

- skill variety (the number of different activities which the job requires);
- task identity (the degree to which an identifiable piece of work is required);
- task significance (the impact on others of the job);
- autonomy (the amount of independence the employee has); and
- task feedback (the information about employee performance obtained from the job).

Their job characteristics model (JCM) has informed subsequent thinking about job design, leading to the recommendation that jobs should be 'enriched' in order to promote increased satisfaction and performance, and reduce absenteeism and labour turnover. Job enrichment entailed greater autonomy and responsibility.

Karasek (1979) proposed that jobs which entailed high control or decision latitude (i.e. autonomy) were more beneficial for the employee in terms of psychological strain. Control over important decisions about one's workplace was hypothesised to change or moderate the way workload in a job is perceived. Jobs that were demanding in terms of workload, yet high in affording control, were suggested to be less stressful than similar jobs low in control. Pierce and Newstrom (1983) showed that 'flexitime' – that is, having some influence over when to start and finish work – led to decreased stress. Wall and Clegg (1981) showed that increased workgroup autonomy in how to complete tasks produced improvements in employee well-being.

Job redesign and performance

The effect of initiatives to enrich jobs on performance, in contrast to their effect on job satisfaction and well-being, has been difficult to demonstrate with any consistency. Sometimes benefits have been found, sometimes not (Kelly, 1992). Thus two key questions arise: what are the circumstances under which job redesign does and does not enhance performance, and what is the explanation for this effect when it does arise?

A possible answer can be found in research on modern computer-controlled manufacturing systems. In terms of performance, the key feature of AMT systems is that when functioning normally they have a fixed capacity: they produce a given amount to a given quality standard. Performance, therefore, is a direct function of failure of the system to operate as planned, of stoppages or malfunctions of the production process due to such factors as mechanical devices moving out of tolerance, computer program bugs or problems with the sensors which provide electronic information to the computers. AMT installations are prone to such faults because of their speed, range and complexity of operation. By the same token, faults typically carry high economic costs. Thus error management is placed at centre stage in the manufacturing process, and raises the issue of what form of job design minimises operating errors.

In cases where operators' jobs have been 'enriched', the effect of operator job redesign on AMT performance has been found to depend on system variability or 'technological uncertainty'. For predictable, reliable and typically less complex systems, there is little or no direct performance benefit from introducing wider responsibilities for operators. Where frequent operating difficulties arise, both from factors intrinsic to the technology and from the need to adapt the technology to changing demands, job redesign has been shown to produce substantial performance improvements.

Wall *et al.* (1991) studied operators of computer numeric controlled (CNC) machines used in the assembly of printed circuit boards. Their original jobs were of the simplified kind described above, but were redesigned to encompass tasks previously undertaken by specialists. To this end operators were trained in fault rectification during a period of two weeks. They were shown how to recalibrate mechanisms that worked out of tolerance, reset mechanisms and edit programs to cope with variations in raw materials, and to carry out a range of other relevant activities. They were then required (and willing) to carry out these new tasks as an integral part of their own jobs. Specialist staff were called upon only in the case of more fundamental difficulties. The findings, based on performance over 50 days before the job change and 50 days after, were unambiguous. In the case of machines characterised by high technological uncertainty, there was a dramatic decrease in downtime and hence a corresponding increase in output.

The preceding discussion suggests that giving operators some opportunity to decide how and when to intervene in the running of the AMT system allows them to use job-related knowledge and skills relevant to system performance. It has also been argued that increased autonomy produces a change in the way in which operators view the nature of their job, to more proactive 'role orientations'. Examples of this type of role orientation include being more aware of, and concerned about, customer and team goals, and being more proactive in seeking out and preventing faults, rather than narrowly focused on just following established procedures in doing the job. The proposal is that such role orientations are also important to performance, but as yet there is no empirical evidence for this link.

It has been argued that the modern manufacturing initiatives outlined above have increased the importance of other aspects of jobs. Two in particular have been discussed (see Parker and Wall, 1996): cognitive demand and production responsibility. Cognitive demand is further divided into attentional demand and problem-solving demand. Attentional demand refers to passive monitoring aspects of jobs, and problem-solving demand refers to more active problem-solving and fault prevention. Production responsibility refers to the fact that JIT means that disruptions to production are more visible, and result in machine downtime which carries a production cost.

Martin and Wall (1989) showed that psychological strain was related to cognitive demand and production responsibility in AMT installations. Operators whose jobs were high on both aspects experienced strain, whereas jobs high on one or the other aspect did not produce negative effects.

Finally, the broad picture of research into the effects of job design is that research has followed practice. Thus job design research is the child of organisational development and management initiatives, rather than their companion. What this means is that it is likely that not all the job characteristics important to feelings of satisfaction, well-being and performance have been identified, and linked to a theoretical framework. Indeed, in studies in industrial settings it is often impossible to attribute psychological outcomes to any particular job-related cause, because change in one job characteristic is usually accompanied by changes in others. Different characteristics are probably differentially important in different industrial contexts.

Job analysis

Job analysis could be regarded as a logical companion to scientific management. In order to determine what can be done, and how efficiently, it is necessary to analyse the components of a job. With the decline of scientific management, the interest in job analysis also declined, being used largely to set wage levels. However, there has been renewed interest since the 1970s because of the need to try to compare different types of job in order to evaluate their comparative worth. This relates to equal pay for people who do different jobs, but who carry out work that draws on similar knowledge or level of responsibility. Another reason for an interest in job analysis is that analysing the requirements for a job means that the abilities needed to do the job can be determined, and then used in picking a suitable person for the job. Using job analysis can help in setting salary levels, and in highlighting any unfair discrimination in selection, for example in the standards being set for recruiting, and in the procedures being used to make selection decisions. However, understanding what a job consists of forms a central plank to many other activities. It can be the basis for making decisions about job descriptions, critical job needs, the pay level relative to other jobs, the staffing levels needed, the training required, the performance to be expected from job-holders, and the consequent assessments for promotion or continued employment.

Job analysis itself is concerned primarily in identifying those responsibilities and tasks that constitute a job. In order to do this, information about the jobs has to be gathered and analysed. The information can be collected through a variety of means, for example by interviewing those in the job, by looking at written job descriptions, by asking subordinates, peers and superiors, and through direct observation of the person at work.

Several methods have been proposed, but for space reasons not all of them will be described. The ones that will be outlined here are chosen to give a broad view of the kinds of approach that can be taken to job analysis.

Functional job analysis

Functional job analysis attempts to identify job tasks, set performance standards and delineate the training needs of workers. It relies on trained persons to use interviews with workers, training and other materials, and observation to analyse jobs using five components: first, purposes, goals and objectives; second, specific tasks; third, abilities required; fourth, performance standards; and fifth, training needs. The abilities needed are related to data handling, communication, machines, language, mathematics, reasoning and autonomy in the job.

A related system is the position analysis questionnaire (PAQ) (McCormick *et al.*, 1972), which analysts use to classify jobs according to six dimensions: information input; mental processes; work output; interpersonal activities; work situation; and miscellaneous. Rating scales are used which look at the extent, importance, time, applicability, and so on, of the dimensions to jobs. The PAQ attempts to provide a method of analysing any job. Job analysts use the PAQ as the basis for structured interviews of workers and supervisors. From these interviews a job element profile is identified, and this can be used to draw up a job description and compare different jobs. Thereafter a profile of the attributes needed to perform the elements can be produced. The attributes consist of the aptitudes, interests and temperament required for the job, and can be used to detail a person specification for the job. The attribute profile allows recommendations for the types of psychological tests which will assess the attributes in a person, and aid the selection of the right person for the job.

The PAQ is one of the most-researched approaches to job analysis. For example, responses from job-holders have been compared to those from supervisors, and found to be in fairly good agreement, thus demonstrating some convergent validity. However, other findings show that naive raters, often using job titles or written job descriptions, also show good agreement with job experts. These observations naturally raise questions about the basis for expert analysts' judgements: are they based on stereotypes or actual job factors?

The PAQ technique was developed in the USA. A related approach developed in the UK is the job components inventory (JCI) (Banks, 1988).

A different approach is to analyse jobs not in terms of generalised job and worker characteristics, but through specific reference to actual job behaviour.

Critical incidents technique

The critical incidents method is based on asking workers for examples of on-the-job behaviours or critical incidents which were either extremely effective or ineffective in realising the objectives of the job. Once collected, incidents are grouped by raters into job functions incorporating particular job responsibilities. The job elements approach is similar but tries to identify job elements such as skills, knowledge, abilities, willingness, interest and personal qualities necessary to do a specific job. Other approaches to job analysis have focused on the physical and human abilities needed to do a job.

Whatever the centre of interest, however, job analyses encounter several problems. First, jobs are often changing, and this is particularly so with the introduction of computerised technology, the trend towards team-based working and the associated drive towards more flexible jobs. Thus a job analysis may be out of date before it can be used effectively. Second, the analysis is only as good as the sources of information on which it is based, and often this boils down to subjective opinion. Third, like any measure, a job analysis should be examined for reliability and validity. This is rarely done, and would be very time-consuming to do, as well as costing a lot of money. Despite these problems there are benefits to be had through analysing jobs. Job evaluation is a method by which jobs are ranked with respect to their value to an organisation, and this value is often reflected in the salary paid for doing that job. The salary can also be set according to market rates based on economic factors, of course. If the salary is influenced by what the job contains, however, then a job analysis can identify the skills and responsibilities which should be rewarded by pay.

Task analysis

The approaches to job analysis outlined above are rather general when it comes to considering how people deal with computerised technology in their jobs. The techniques, in principle, are fine as far as they go, in breaking jobs down into what workers do, and what abilities and skill levels they need to possess. There are, though, many more considerations to take into account when a job depends on using computers to control and operate complex machinery and systems. In this context the nature of the tasks using the computer becomes important, the sequencing and timing of tasks can be crucial to success, and the amount of mental effort required to perform well needs to be identified to avoid over-loading limited cognitive resources such as memory and attention.

To understand the detail of tasks involving machines, techniques have been developed which come under the rubric of **task analysis**. Shepherd (1996, p. 145) describes task analysis as dealing with 'issues associated with the performance of human beings interacting with tools, plant, equipment, other human beings, and the world at large'. The description is all-encompassing in one sense, and there are clear overlaps with job analysis, but there is a key element which helps differentiate task analysis from more general job analytic approaches. The key element is the focus on performance. Task analysis is concerned primarily with workers doing things, not job content, 'Task analysis should examine what people are required to do and the constraints that are placed on them' (Shepherd, 1996, p. 145). So task analysis has been used to examine industrial accidents or failure to meet production targets, and to design human–machine interfaces, as well as to design training and jobs.

Task analysis can be traced back to early work study methods. Work study methods were concerned with observing and timing work actions, mostly in connection with manual skills. The aim was to devise ways of working which reduced the time taken to carry out tasks. A famous example is the lifting and loading of pig iron studied by Frederick Taylor just before the turn of the century, and mentioned above. Taylor managed vastly to increase the efficiency with which pig iron was dealt with, saving time and hence increasing productivity. His scheme of 'scientific management' was largely founded on the detailed analysis of tasks and activities. Work study has been most closely associated with repetitive tasks, such as those found on assembly lines. It tended to focus on performance, like meeting production targets, to the exclusion of other factors such as cognition, occupational health and job satisfaction. Modern-day manufacturing relies much more on integrated production methods which require workers to monitor their activity, plan strategies and make decisions.

Modern-day task analysis incorporates psychological factors, using models of how people handle and process mental information. Thus memory, learning, attention, mental effort, and decision-making are factors considered. A common approach, influenced by R.B. Miller (e.g. 1962), sets out to detail, somewhat confusingly, two main stages of task analysis: task description and task analysis.

Task description is a statement of what an operator has to do in his or her job put into system or operational terms. The description is concerned with how the system state is changed. For example, imagine you are an air traffic controller. Your job is to guide aircraft to land safely on the airport runway. You do this by tracking the movements of aircraft in your sector on a radar screen in front of you, and issuing instructions to pilots by radio communications.

A hypothetical task description might start with: 'turn on the radar'; 'adjust screen brightness'; 'test microphone sensitivity', and so on. A common theme with this and many other ways of analysing tasks, is that the task description is hierarchical. 'Turn on the radar' and 'adjust screen brightness' are part of 'maintain the radar system'. Lower-order descriptors are nested within higher-order descriptors. That is, in order to fulfil a higher-level descriptor, the lower-order descriptors must be carried out.

Any hierarchical system must convey how the lower-order descriptors are organised in order to fulfil the higher-level function. Thus 'turning the radar on' must happen before 'adjusting screen brightness'. There are a number of ways of representing order. A common representation, used in functional task analysis, is to represent functional activities in the form of a map going from left to right across a page, with the higher-order functions on the left.

Task analysis is concerned with a behavioural analysis of the structure of tasks. A behavioural analysis could (and often does) structure behaviour in terms of the information processing of the air traffic controller. So the behavioural analysis might include 'receive information on aircraft position'; 'interpret information received'; 'decide appropriate course of action'; and 'speak to pilot'.

Miller took a pragmatic approach to task analysis. He was not concerned to test any specific view of human information processing, but wished to provide a practical framework for exploring various influences on performance. For example, controlling a complex process such as the generation of electricity involves many simple activities such as monitoring instruments, opening and closing valves, and operating pumps. However, the order of activities is governed by the need to control the process within safe limits, to a certain quality standard, and in an efficient way. Thus task activity is bound up with judgements and decisions about the way in which performance indicators should be met.

Hierarchical task analysis

Hierarchical task analysis (HTA) was developed in the 1960s and 1970s (Annett and Duncan, 1967; Duncan, 1972) to cope with jobs changes away from physical, repetitive activities, to supervisory, mental, ones such as controlling power generation. The trend has continued with widespread use of computerised technology to control essential aspects of, *inter alia*, power generation and many manufacturing processes. The jobs involve mental rather than physical activity, and operators are more concerned with monitoring the production system than actively controlling it.

Tasks are analysed using HTA by specifying system goals and the operations required to meet them. For example, a goal could be a production target (so many kilowatts of electricity generated per hour, say), and an operation is what a worker does to the system to move it towards its goal (for example, increasing the rate at which fuel is used to produce the electricity).

Goals can be viewed in two different ways: by the human–task interaction, or by redescription. The human–task interaction considers operations in terms of input, action and feedback (IAF). Competence at an operation suggests an ability to collect information relevant to the task, an ability to act on the system to move it towards the goal state, and an ability to monitor appropriate feedback concerning the execution of the correct action, and its effect on the system. Redescription, on the other hand, analyses a goal in terms of subgoals and the way in which they should be organised (called a plan) in order to achieve the goal.

Although HTA has been presented as a modern way of looking at complex tasks, there are several points to note. First, it is a pragmatic framework, so it should be judged on whether it works or not. It is not particularly located in psychological principles, but relies to some extent on the strategic and intuitive abilities of the analyst. Second, if several tasks have to be done in the same time slot HTA cannot, by itself, determine whether this will cause problems: some tasks are prompted by instructions or rules to be followed, and others are determined by states of the system at any one time. A third point to consider is how far an analyst needs to go in using HTA. Annett and Duncan (1967) suggest that goals and operations should not be analysed unless performance is seen as unacceptable. One of the useful features of HTA is that it can be deployed to consider all potential problems in a proposed system before job, task and equipment design work begins.

Job satisfaction and well-being

Work is a large part of life for those in employment. An important part of work, therefore, is the enjoyment to be gained from it, and the consequences of such satisfaction for job performance as well as feelings of well-being. The research on job satisfaction is not specifically directed at working with technology, but clearly the research is relevant to any job, including those reliant on modern technology.

Job satisfaction can be viewed as an all-embracing attitude or feeling (that is, a worker can be questioned about his or her overall approach to their job), or it can be seen as the amalgamation of many different attitudes to specific parts of a job, such as the type of work, working conditions, workmates, company policy and promotion opportunities. A more manageable characterisation is to distinguish betweeen 'intrinsic' and 'extrinsic' job satisfaction. 'Intrinsic' satisfaction concerns aspects related to doing the job; for example, amount of autonomy, the skills needed and task variety. 'Extrinsic' satisfaction relates to those job aspects surrounding the job, such as pay, working conditions and job security.

Job-related well-being has been viewed as including job satisfaction, but also feelings of anxiety or comfort, and feelings of enthusiasm or depression (e.g. Warr, 1996). Research has shown that job-specific well-being is correlated with feelings of overall well-being. The relationship appears to be interdependent: job-specific well-being affects overall well-being and vice versa.

Job features which have a bearing on well-being have been delineated by Warr (1987), and placed into nine groups:

- opportunity for personal control (e.g. autonomy and participation in decision-making);
- opportunity for skill use (e.g. skills needed and use of skills);
- variety (e.g. non-repetitive work);
- job goals (e.g. workload and responsibility);
- environmental clarity (e.g. feedback and information about what is required);
- physical security (e.g. safe working conditions and well-designed equipment);
- opportunity for contact with other people (e.g. good relationships and communications);
- availability of money (e.g. salary and budgets);
- valued social position (e.g. status of the job and job meaningfulness).

The perspective from the employer's standpoint is focused on productivity, quality of work, absenteeism and staff turnover. All these have a direct bearing on the profitability of the company. An interesting question is whether job satisfaction has any influence on productivity, quality, and so on. Reports which have looked at a meta-analysis of many studies of the relationship of job satisfaction to job performance (often measured by supervisors' ratings) have shown that the relationship is a weakish one. The relationship has been observed to be stronger for intrinsic than extrinsic satisfaction (Iaffaldano and Muchinsky, 1985), and stronger in managerial and professional workers (Petty *et al.*, 1984).

Relationships of job satisfaction to other aspects of work have also been observed. Muchinsky and Tuttle (1979) found a negative correlation with staff turnover (i.e. higher satisfaction was associated with lower turnover and vice versa), and Clegg (1983) observed that increases in tardiness and absenteeism were accompanied by increases in job dissatisfaction. The factors just mentioned are expensive for organisations. Turnover means that further recruitment and training need to be done, and lateness and absenteeism mean lost production. Organisations have tried to increase employee satisfaction, therefore, through a variety of ways. Job enrichment, based on the job characteristics model of Hackman and Oldham (1976), gives workers extra responsibility. Job enlargement gives workers additional tasks to do. Other ways relate to the salary structure and profit-sharing for employees. The general idea of these schemes is to involve workers more closely with the organisation, and satisfy their job-related needs. They are close cousins of motivational schemes at work.

Job-related stress

Work pressures, deadlines, overwork, difficult colleagues or impossible job demands can all affect how a worker feels about his or her job. The feeling of being under strain is a negative consequence, whereas the feeling of being challenged and meeting those challenges is positive. Thus the impact of work-related stressors and a person's reaction to them is moderated by how they are perceived.

It is difficult to judge the precise impact of stress at work, but estimates suggest that approximately half of all working days lost in the USA through absenteeism are stress-related (Elkin and Rosch, 1990). A similar figure has been mooted for the UK.

Different views of conceptualising stress have been proposed. A commonly held approach is to consider demands in a job or aspects of the working environment as stressors, which can place a person under strain. The person's ability to cope with and/or adapt to work demands influences how much strain is felt (O'Driscoll and Cooper, 1996).

Another way of viewing stress is as a physiological reaction to environmental stressors. Selye (1936, 1976) identified a common 'fight or flight' nervous system response to a variety of physical and mental stressors. The response included increased heart and respiratory rate, and sweating. Selye called the response the general adaptation syndrome (GAS). One of the GAS's most important aspects is that the physiological system acts to bring the body back to a state of equilibrium following experience of a stressor. However, if the stressor continues to act, or the body's defence mechanisms do not work properly, then the body moves into a stage of 'exhaustion' where adaptive mechanisms do not function fully and distress follows.

Job-related stress is often seen in the context of a person–environment (P–E) fit model (French et al., 1982). The model proposes that strain results where there is a mismatch between the person and the environment on dimensions important to the well-being of the worker. Thus the central idea is that there is an optimal level of environmental demand that matches an individual's capabilities. Mismatches can occur where a job is boring or too demanding.

Psychological strain at work is often measured using questionnaires. The reasons for this are often to do with the ease of using questionnaires as compared with other methods. One of the most frequently used measures is the general health questionnaire (GHQ), which asks about the ability to concentrate on tasks, sleep difficulties, feelings of strain, enjoyment, unhappiness and depression. **Physiological measures**, such as increased heart rate, blood pressure, blood cholesterol and urinary catecholamines, are often more difficult to collect. There are, however, several advantages to physiological measures as compared with questionnaires. They are less subject to biases in self-reports since they do not rely on subjective recall or descriptions of stress symptoms, and they offer potentially greater discrimination between different levels of stress. Cooper *et al.* (1988) suggest that certain occupations such as police work, advertising and mining have the highest stress levels. However, since jobs are always changing, albeit at different rates, particularly with the introduction of new technology, it is probably impossible to generate a stable ranking of the most stressful jobs.

One approach to job-related stress is to try to identify work characteristics which are associated with, or predict, stress.

Specific aspects of jobs (called intrinsic job characteristics) identified through research as stressors are lack of variety, monotonous work and absence of discretion and control. In addition, factors in the physical working environment, such as excessive heat or noise, have been shown to influence well-being. Karasek (1979) has argued that jobs with high demands, but with low control or decision latitude over when and how those demands are met, are particularly stressful.

Other work-related sources of psychological strain include: role ambiguity, role conflict and role overload. Role ambiguity involves the unpredictability of the consequences of a person's role performance, and the lack of information regarding expected role behaviours. Role conflict concerns incompatible demands on a person, and role overload refers to the number of different roles a person has (O'Driscoll and Cooper, 1996).

At the extreme, workers can experience 'burnout', a process whereby increased work demands lead to emotional exhaustion, followed by an insensitive attitude to others at work, and finally to feelings of low self-achievement, frustration and helplessness (Jackson *et al.*, 1986). Burnout is characterised by becoming less committed, withdrawing from the job, and can lead to increased tardiness and absenteeism. It has been found to be prevalent in occupations which involve the care of others, for example social work, nursing and police work. Research suggests that the development of burnout is associated with high levels of contact with people, especially related to dealing with their problems (Cordes and Dougherty, 1993).

Consistent with the person–environment view, Weiman (1977) studied over 1500 managers and found that having too much or too little to do, having unclear or inflexible job demands, having too much or no role conflict, and having no or a very high level of responsibility led to the incidence of hypertension and heart disease amongst other health-related outcomes.

There is a widespread belief that many physical illnesses are stress-related, including ulcers, heart disease, migraines and hypertension (Beehr and Bhagat, 1985). Research has implicated stress in effects on the immune system (Dienstbier, 1989).

Individuals can differ in their response to stressors. Type A personalities (Friedman and Rosenman, 1974) are characterised as hard-driving, having a chronic sense of time urgency, and impatient with obstacles in their way. Type B personalities, on the other hand, are viewed as relaxed, satisfied and unhurried. Research suggests that type A people are at greater risk of suffering heart attacks and strokes.

Other theorists (e.g. Lazarus and Folkman, 1984) propose that a key aspect of whether the person experiences strain depends on how the situation is viewed by the individual. Cognitive appraisal is the term used by Lazarus, and it is conceptualised as having three components: primary, secondary and reappraisal. Primary appraisal is where the person evaluates an environmental event as important for his or her well-being. Secondary appraisal involves the person assessing how or whether he or she can deal with the situation. Reappraisal is an evaluation of whether the coping strategies adopted have been successful.

Lazarus and Folkman (1984) categorise coping strategies into two types: problem-focused and emotion-focused. Problem-focused approaches act to reduce stressors or minimise their effect, whereas emotion-focused approaches involve reducing the psychological and/or emotional consequences of the stressors. Strategies to cope with stress at work include changing the situation; denying, distorting or repressing unpleasant aspects of reality; changing expectations so that desires match the situation; reducing the importance of the work situation; and using physical exercise, diet and relaxation techniques to make oneself feel better (Edwards, 1992).

Research has not shown a consistent picture with regard to coping strategies. There have been problems in how to measure strategies appropriately, and there is a question over whether individuals have a consistent coping style, or whether they adapt or cope differently depending on the stressful situation they find themselves in. There is no clear consensus about which ways of coping are effective for different types of stressors.

Employees may have a limited opportunity to adopt some coping strategies. Jobs where work is determined by machine – for example, jobs on computer-controlled production lines – can afford relatively little control over when and how tasks are carried out. To change the nature of such jobs requires change at the organisational level, for example through job redesign.

Work-related strategies targeted at the source of stress include time management techniques and job rotation. At the organisational level some companies have introduced stress management courses for their employees. Matteson and Ivancevich (1987) propose that effective stress management programmes should impart knowledge, skills and attitudes that are useful in coping with stressors. An alternative or complementary perspective is to alter the jobs that employees do, or change the organisational structure so that employees have adequate training, have a sense of control over their work, are not subject to punitive management, do not work in unnecessarily dangerous conditions, and are facilitated in communicating effectively with others in the organisation. In the USA a 'quality of work life' movement, incorporating these ideas, was begun in the 1970s, and early studies suggested that there were increases in productivity and quality as a result (Herrick and Maccoby, 1975).

Murphy (1988) identified three levels of organisational intervention in stress management: primary, where stressors, for example workload, are reduced; secondary, where employees are helped to reappraise their situation, for example through stress management programmes; and tertiary, where employees are helped to deal with the results of stress, for example through employee assistance programmes (EAPs). The majority of organ-isation-led interventions occur at the secondary and tertiary levels, and offer training and counselling to employees. The effectiveness of such interventions has yet to be convincingly demonstrated.

There have been very few studies of change at the primary level. However, job changes which increase employee participa-tion in decision-making, introduce more flexible work schedules, and increase job autonomy have been shown to reduce employee strain (Parker *et al.*, 1997).

Summary

This chapter has outlined the main approaches to job design, job and task analysis, job satisfaction and job-related stress. Job design is concerned with aspects of jobs which are applicable, in principle, to a broad range of jobs. Research has identified several characteristics of jobs important for psychological well-being. The relationship of job design to performance is less well understood. Job analysis seeks to describe, through standard procedures, the content of jobs and the abilities required to do them. Task analysis is concerned with the detailed nature of tasks and their sequencing. Both approaches adopt a pragmatic perspective. Job satisfaction was considered in relation to feelings of well-being. Finally, job-related stress and its potential consequences for health were considered, and organisational and individual coping with stress consequences discussed.

Chapter 3

Technology and personnel

- Skill acquisition   40
- Training   43
  Training needs   44
  Training programmes   44
  Behavioural theories   45
  Cognitive theories   45
  Training evaluation   46
  Training for technology in the future   46
- Personnel selection   48
  Interviews   50
  Employment testing   51
- Performance appraisal   54
  Appraisal methods   55
- Motivation at work   58
  Maslow's need hierarchy   58
  McClelland's 'need for achievement'
     theory   59
  Herzberg's two-factor theory   60
  Job characteristics model   61
  Equity theory of motivation   62
  Expectancy or VIE theory   62
- Summary   63

THIS CHAPTER OUTLINES the main aspects of matching people to jobs and tasks. Often this function has been treated under the rubric of personnel work. New technology has not altered the basic personnel function at one level: organisations still need to recruit, appraise and motivate people for the jobs they are required to do. What has changed, of course, is the abilities required to use new technology and to carry out tasks related to it. The skills needed are more likely to be mental than physical ones. Key considerations, therefore, are how best to increase relevant job- and task-related knowledge and cognitive skills, and what **mental capabilities** are required for using the new technology. The former is a question of training and skill acquisition, and the latter a question of choosing and developing the people with the needed abilities. The chapter begins with skill acquisition and training rather than personnel selection and recruitment, owing to the obvious, but perhaps overlooked, fact that new technology and attendant changes in work practices and tasks demand the learning and acquiring of new skills and techniques. Organisations will not be able to select appropriate people if they do not have the required skills, and those already in employment will be required to learn new knowledge and skills for the organisation to remain competitive.

Skill acquisition

New technology, and in particular technology involving computer control and communication, places special demands on mental activity on the part of those operating the system. Thus memory, decision-making and problem-solving skills become much more important to success than hitherto.

Skill has been defined as co-ordinated activity to achieve a goal, in terms of fluency, accuracy and speed. It involves knowing how to carry out a task. A key aspect of skilled behaviour is its adaptability to new situations and changing task requirements. It has been estimated that it takes a long time to become proficient at learning cognitive-based skills, and even longer to become an expert (Anderson, 1982).

Learning a skill has been observed often to follow a power law. For example, Crossman (1959) found that female operators learning to make cigars improved quickly to start with, but then performance increased relatively slowly, until it more or less plateaued. Patrick (1992) details three possible explanations for the power law effect in learning: the mixed components model; the selection model; and the exhaustion model. The mixed components model proposes that some parts of the task could be learned more quickly, leaving the slower components to be learned over time. The selection model argues that practice could increase the likelihood that the optimal way of doing the task will be arrived at. Finally, the exhaustion model suggests that learning will decrease with practice because there is less room for further improvement. It is possible that these explanations are not mutually exclusive, and could apply together.

A second broad observation about skill acquisition is that it depends on feedback about how a person is succeeding at the task. Two types of feedback can be distinguished: intrinsic, which is a consequence of the normal execution of the task; and extrinsic, which is not normally available, such as instruction.

Many studies of cognitively based skills have considered how novices differ from experts in order to discover how information processing changes with skill acquisition. The tasks studied have included chess and computer operation. Chi *et al.* (1988) summarise the attributes of experts as: excelling mainly in their own domain of expertise; perceiving large meaningful patterns in their domain; being fast and relatively error-free in task execution; representing problems at a deep level, not tied to surface aspects of the task; spending time analysing a problem qualitatively; possessing developed self-monitoring skills; and having superior short- and long-term memory.

Elements of these observations have been incorporated into views of good work performance based on better mental understanding. For example, Frese and Zapf (1993) explain the idea of a 'superworker' based on studies of people at work and using computer simulation problems. Superworkers were more realistic about the time for a task to be done; they showed less activity but produced more; and the best managers anticipated more problems, appreciated more implications, and predicted events more accurately. In a series of studies Dörner asked people to control complex computer simulations, for example acting as the mayor of a small German town. He found that successful subjects had more precise goals, asked more questions, planned more, developed and tested more hypotheses, made more decisions, had more goals and were more self-reflective. There was no difference in IQ between successful and less successful subjects. In short, Frese and Zapf suggest that superworkers have a better mental understanding of a job, and better work strategies, and that motivation is not the factor that discriminates superworkers from others.

The dominant theories of skill acquisition stem from an analysis put forward by Fitts (1962). He suggested, on the basis of experiments, the opinions of pilot trainers and the views of sports coaches, that there are three phases. The first phase he termed the cognitive phase, and this includes learning formal procedures and rules. What is learned can be articulated, and performance is relatively error-prone. The second phase is called the associative phase, where correct behaviour is established through practice and errors are gradually eliminated. The third phase is called the autonomous phase, where speed of performance increases, and performance becomes increasingly resistant to stress and interference.

More recently Anderson (1983, 1987) has put forward a three-stage theory which utilises two key concepts. The first concerns declarative and procedural knowledge. **Declarative knowledge** is factual knowledge that can be stated (i.e. knowing that . . .). **Procedural knowledge** is knowledge about how to do something, which may not be verbalisable (i.e. knowing how . . .). The second concept is production rules. Production rules have the form IF condition X is met THEN execute Y: for example, IF the goal is to start the car and the fuel gauge reads empty THEN fill the fuel tank with petrol.

Anderson's three stages are declarative, knowledge compilation and tuning stages. The declarative stage involves the learner having facts about a new task, and using these and general problem-solving to perform the task. In the knowledge compilation stage declarative knowledge is translated into procedural knowledge using two processes. The first is composition, where rules are merged or collapsed to form more direct rules, and the second is proceduralisation, where rules are created to take account of context. The third, tuning, stage uses feedback whereby rules become more applicable, and better rules predominate. Knowledge, therefore, progresses from declarative to procedural. (See Anderson, 1995, for a fuller account.)

Skilled performance is usually viewed as hierarchically organised so that components of skill are controlled at a higher level. For example, when learning tennis, a beginner may have to think through every phase of a forehand, consciously deciding where to place his or her foot, how the distribution of weight between the feet should be, where and at what angle the racket should be, and so on. Once skilled, the tennis player merely decides where the ball should be placed to win the point. As skill increases so control passes to higher and higher levels. Once practised, skill components become automatic, and hence require low attentional resources. Controlled processing still requires resources. Another distinction made is between closed- and open-loop control. Closed-loop control is dependent on feedback of discrete actions, in contrast to open-loop, which is a more predictive type of control.

Training

In order to bring about the development of new knowledge and skills, organisations mount programmes aimed at the required information and techniques. The means whereby this is achieved is usually called training, especially if the learning programme is

43

formally instituted by the employing organisation. Training at work can usually be divided into two types: on-the-job training and classroom-based training. On-the-job training can take the form of apprenticeship schemes on the one hand, and informal tuition from an experienced colleague on the other. Classroom-based instruction involves not so much showing the trainee how to perform a particular skill as explaining why things work, and giving instruction in how things ought to be done.

Training needs

Prior to successful training programmes lies an analysis of the needs the programme is designed to meet. If training needs are not identified beforehand, it is impossible to evaluate the value of training later. Training needs can, and perhaps should, incorporate different levels in an organisation. Three main levels are organisation, task and person. Organisational analysis concerns issues such as the parts of the organisation that need training, in light of the short- and long-term goals of the organisation, the cost-effectiveness of the training, and the commitment to training on the part of employees. The task level concerns the knowledge, skills and abilities needed by employees to perform specific jobs. The requirements for a specific job can be derived from a job description generated through a job analysis. The person level is concerned with individual employees and their capabilities. The latter can be determined from performance appraisal systems, recruitment tests for new workers, and from workers' self-assessment of their own training needs. Individual training provides the opportunity for individual development at work.

Training programmes

The way in which training programmes are organised and run is often the product of experience as to what works, rather than being based on strong scientific learning principles. There is therefore a gap between theory and practice which hopefully will narrow in the future. The training process has several parts:

identification of training needs and objectives; development of training materials; and implementation and evaluation of the training programme. Certain practical constraints can guide this process. Training needs can be set in relation to organisational goals and current effectiveness, a task analysis focused on what the trainees need to learn, and the background and abilities of the trainees themselves. Training objectives should be measurable rather than vague aspirations. Specific goals will help job performance and learning (Latham *et al.*, 1982). The general aim of many training programmes is to facilitate an employee's learning, retention and transfer of job-related skills.

Although training at work often is guided by experience on the part of trainers, there are several theories of learning based in psychology which can provide some assistance. These theories could be considered as falling into two main categories: behavioural and cognitive.

Behavioural theories

Behavioural theories encompass classical (Pavlov) and operant (Skinner) conditioning, and social learning theory (Bandura, 1977). In essence the ideas contained in these theories are that reflex behaviour can be conditioned to different types of stimuli, that behaviours are learned and maintained by being rewarded, and that behaviours can be learned by observing and imitating another person's actions. Thus training programmes could make use of paired associations, rewards and punishments, and role modelling and videotapes.

Cognitive theories

Cognitive theories are based on the study of skill acquisition in people, and concentrate on the knowledge and abilities gained through the learning experience. The way in which knowledge is acquired and whether it is transferable forms the focus, and considers whether knowledge is declarative or procedural, automatic or requiring conscious effort to implement (see Stammers, 1996, for further discussion). Thus training programmes could consider whether a trainee is an expert or novice, how they organise their knowledge, whether they are able to articulate their knowledge, and hence transfer it across different job contexts, and whether employees have the understanding necessary to handle the complexity of modern, technologically based jobs.

Training evaluation

There is a common perception amongst writers on training that not much evaluation of training is done, and that when it is done, evaluation is frequently rudimentary, often merely gaining the reactions of trainees (Patrick, 1992). This is surprising given that training costs money and involves time away from the job.

Evaluation of training depends on a clear understanding of why the training was done, what goals it met, individual and organisational, how its effectiveness was measured, what resources were allocated, and what was expected of the training programme. In short, training needs should have been identified against which the effects of training can be compared.

There are a variety of frameworks within which training effects can be evaluated (see Patrick, 1992, for an extended discussion). Important are the criteria needed to assess training effects. The main measures include those based on trainee impressions including their enjoyment of the training, and its perceived value; those concerned with how much has been learned through training, often measured through tests of some kind; those which concentrate on the new skills demonstrated on the job – that is, the transfer of training to the job; and those which centre on organisational objectives such as increased production, or production quality.

Training for technology in the future

Traditionally, training is constituted by a trainer providing some formal knowledge to the trainee, whether when doing the job or in the classroom, which is then developed into a skill through practice. However, this perspective is being increasingly challenged by arguments that competitive edge and new technology are also served by the use of knowledge which may not be 'teachable' by formal, instruction-based methods because the knowledge is connected with how to do tasks and cannot be readily articulated and communicated.

In Chapter 2 a study by Wall *et al.* (1991) of operators of computer numeric controlled (CNC) machines used in the assembly of printed circuit boards was discussed. There it was reported that performance benefits had accrued as a result of job redesigns which gave the operators more control over the technology.

Qualitative data suggested that the improved system performance reflected two very different underlying processes: an initial application of existing knowledge, where the mandate to rectify faults necessarily brought benefits (i.e. a quick response effect); and a subsequent development of predictive knowledge. A reanalysis of the data from the study by Jackson and Wall (1991) provided additional support for the two explanations. They argued that the most obvious explanation (as originally assumed) was that improvements in downtime could be accounted for by a quicker response to system faults. With operators responsible for rectifying faults, and on hand when they arose, downtime previously incurred through waiting for specialists was eliminated. This meant, of course, that there should be just as many faults, but on average they would be of shorter duration. This explanation did not appear sufficient to explain the size of the overall effect, however. So an alternative was considered: that part of the performance improvement resulted from fault prevention. The evidence supported this second explanation, showing that a major factor in the overall improvement in system performance was a reduction in the incidence of faults. Moreover, the reduction did not materialise immediately following the job redesign, as would be expected if it involved the application of existing knowledge. Instead there was gradual improvement which reached an asymptote only after many weeks. Thus whilst the operators had been given the authority to rectify faults, it was evident that they had also learned to prevent them. Equivalent findings have been reported by Wall *et al.* (1992)

in a study of a robotics line. Their results also showed that increased operator responsibility for fault rectification (in this case without formal training) was followed by improved system performance, which materialised only after some time.

Chmiel and Wall (1994) have argued that the predictive knowledge which allowed operators to prevent faults was acquired without much conscious thought, leading to knowledge about fault prevention which cannot be readily articulated. Knowledge of this sort has been called 'implicit' (e.g. Broadbent, 1990). Implicit knowledge is defined as being relatively non-verbal and inaccessible to conscious processes, in contrast to explicit knowledge, which is readily explainable to others. Implicit learning depends, in part, on how obvious cause and effect relationships are in a system. If the relationships are not obvious, or expected, then learning tends to be implicit.

The plausibility that implicit knowledge could underlie effective AMT fault management has been demonstrated by Gardner *et al.* (1996) using a simulation of a robotics manufacturing line, based on the study by Wall *et al.* (1992) mentioned above. Gardner *et al.* (1996) showed that learning to diagnose faults produced by the simulation was a function of how obvious or 'salient' the relationship between a fault and its causes was. Causes that were less 'salient' produced knowledge less open to verbal, conscious explanation.

These findings have strong implications for training methods because implicit learning has been shown in the laboratory to depend on 'hands-on' active involvement and experience, rather than instruction-based methods (Berry, 1991). Therefore training in the future may well need to take into account the type of knowledge the training is designed to foster, and the ways in which 'implicitly' learned skills related to technology use are developed.

Personnel selection

The most obvious requirement for a company or organisation is to find the right people to do the jobs and tasks needed to achieve the company goals. New technology has altered the basis for choosing whom to employ. Picking bad employees costs a great deal in wasted time spent on recruiting, training, supervising and sacking that person. Recruiting good employees is essential to success, and so effective selection methods are crucial to this process. The essence of selection is to choose somebody who can confidently be predicted to be able to do the job well, and to get on with others in the organisation. It is not always possible, however, to realise these joint objectives by using a single selection method.

Personnel selection can often appear to be centred on just that moment when a candidate is offered a job. However, to be effective a selection procedure should ideally include a job analysis detailing what is expected of a successful applicant, and a person specification outlining necessary skills, abilities, aptitudes, etc. The essence of the selection process is then to use a method which chooses the right person for the job; that is, the person who will perform in the job as required. Selection tests are measures which afford some prediction of future job behaviour. Their effectiveness as predictors should be judged against indices of job performance, therefore. A good test will predict job performance.

Research supports the idea that selection tests are useful predictors of job performance, but traditional interviews are poor substitutes. Nonetheless, many employers prefer interviews, presumably because of the opportunity interviews provide to assess whether the interviewee will 'fit in'.

The key to the utility and effectiveness of any selection test is that it is both valid and reliable. **Validity** refers to whether the test actually measures what it is supposed to, and **reliability** refers to the consistency with which a test provides results; that is, whether the test measures in the same way time after time, and across different people. There are several types of validity. Criterion-related validity refers to the relationship between the predictor (i.e. selection test score or interview rating) and the criterion (i.e. job performance such as supervisor's ratings or work produced per hour). Criterion-related validity is the most important for job selection. Other types of validity include face validity, which refers to whether a test is 'appropriate' for the job; content validity, which refers to whether the test covers a representative sample of required behaviours; and construct validity, which refers to what the test actually measures.

Interviews

The problems with the job interview as a selection technique are very well documented (see, for example, Anderson and Shackleton, 1993, or Cook, 1993). In general, earlier analyses of research on interviews concluded that they were not a valid or reliable way of identifying good candidates. Interviewers tend to concentrate on negative rather than positive material; training is of limited use in improving interviewer performance; interviewers' impressions may depend more on non-verbal information than on what the candidate is saying. Valid and reliable psychometric tests, for example pencil and paper tests of specific abilities such as reasoning, outperform interviewers in selecting good candidates. For a test to be valid it must measure what it claims to measure, and for it to be reliable the test must measure performance in the same way each time it is used.

Interviews can be done in ways that differ from the traditional wide-ranging discussion of an applicant's background and interests. Panel interviews, where several people question the candidate, improve matters (Landy, 1976), for example. Structuring the interview so that every candidate is asked the same questions improves reliability (Schmitt, 1976). In this type of interview questions and topics outside the structure are not allowed. This does restrict the ability of the interviewer to follow up on interesting areas which arise during the course of the interview. A way round this, which according to Schmitt (1976) also improves reliability, is to use a semi-structured interview, where each candidate is asked about the same broad areas, but supplementary questions can be used to pursue other points as they arise.

More recent views of the interview process (Anderson and Shackleton, 1993) propose that, if appropriate precautions are taken, the interview can hold its own as a selection technique. In particular, if an interview is structured, and based on a detailed job analysis, then reliability and validity are improved. Anderson and Shackleton (1993) also point out that the interview is appropriate for assessing job-relevant social skills.

Another source of information supplied by the candidate is the curriculum vitae (CV). In essence the CV is a record of past experience and achievement, and as such could be a rich source of factual information relevant to the job. However, there is usually no external check on the accuracy of the information on a CV, and it is clearly in a candidate's interest to present him- or herself in the best possible light. In this context references are also often required, but again are problematic regarding their interpretation. At the very least a selector will need to know for how long, and in what capacity, the referee has known the candidate, and what kind of work was undertaken.

The observations on the interview made above are based on research which relates to jobs in general, rather than to the use of new technology in particular. Clearly, there may be problems with using an interview technique as the sole means of choosing someone to operate complex computer-controlled equipment, or even to use electronic means for communication within an organisation. Other techniques, discussed next, are probably more suitable.

Employment testing

The essence of employment testing is to administer a test, or a series of tests, the results of which predict success in the job. Since there are literally hundreds of jobs, there are, as one would expect, a considerable number of tests. These can be grouped under several headings: **ability tests**, personality measures and job sampling.

Ability tests

There are two main subheadings related to ability: mental and physical. Mental ability covers a wide range of tests from those connected to intelligence, through deductive reasoning to spatial and mechanical ability. Deductive reasoning tests examine the person's facility with logic inferences, whereas a test of mechanical ability would examine how the relationship between parts of mechanical objects was understood. Tests of mental ability appear to have the potential for being extremely useful in deciding whether someone will be able to cope with the increasing emphasis on mental skills at work as a consequence of the introduction of new technology. Physical ability tests measure things such as strength, stamina, reaction speed and so on. Tests of ability have been shown to predict performance very well, and so are well validated as a selection tool (Cook, 1993).

Personality measures

You may wonder why personality is considered in selection tests when performance can be assessed through the use of ability tests. Obviously, personal qualities are important in a variety of jobs, and personality measures are used to identify characteristics that are associated with successful performance, and to screen out people who are clearly unsuited to the job. However, the area of personality testing is subject to some controversy, and it remains to be seen whether personality tests achieve the degree of validity and reliability of ability tests in the job selection context.

Job sampling

A job sample is a piece of work provided by the applicant which is considered pertinent to the job being applied for. Examples would be a photographer's portfolio, letters produced by a secretary, and so on. Work already done is used to make judgements about future performance and training needs. A related idea is the work sample test, where applicants are observed carrying out a piece of work related to the job. For example, Campion (1972) devised work sample tests for maintenance mechanics, comprising four tasks: installing pulleys and belts; taking apart and repairing a gearbox; fitting a motor; and preparing a sprocket to fit a shaft.

Another example would be the use of computer technology by a secretary to produce text and picture documents using word processing and graphics applications.

Work sample testing obviously can work only if a person already has the skills necessary to carry out the test. Trainability tests are a form of work sample test which examines how effectively a job applicant can learn a new skill. The instructor gives standardised instructions and a demonstration, and then uses a checklist to rate how well the trainee does.

Although work sample and trainability tests have proved popular with applicants, some analysts have pointed out difficulties with them. Robertson and Downs (1979) reviewed several trainability studies and found that the tests predicted training success better than job performance. Barrett (1992) suggested that work sample tests are uninformative, because they test too many job components at the same time, and they are unlikely to be valid over time because of changes to parts of the job over time. For example, a motor mechanic work sample might test knowledge of carburettors, skill with small tools, and reasoning ability. The work sample does not separate these. If car engines change, for instance with the introduction of fuel injection, then the test loses validity. In the same way a secretary may be skilled at particular types of computer word and graphics processing packages, but may still require intensive training to learn new ones. This point is particularly relevant to this type of technology at work since computer applications, and their capability, have changed dramatically over the last couple of decades.

An assessment centre is a setting where candidates for management posts are observed in group discussions and other exercises designed to produce the kind of behaviours expected of managers. Thus the approach is aimed at observing samples (or a profile) of behaviours related to managing. However, these behaviours are produced during the candidates' time at the assessment centre, and so are not a past record of job-related achievement.

Whichever approach is taken to job samples there is a need for criteria to be established relating to the performance and its interpretation. The key requirement is to relate the job sample to future job performance. This requirement may prove to be unattainable in practice if computer technology continues to drive change in the way in which jobs and tasks are done. A more realistic selection procedure may well focus on mental abilities and trainability in new skills as being more important than knowing how to carry out particular tasks at the time of selection.

Performance appraisal

Performance appraisal is concerned with the criteria, and methods for deriving them, relating to effective job performance, and with the fair means by which individuals can be evaluated against appraisal criteria or standards. Appraisal schemes can be used to decide promotions, salary levels and training needs, set job goals, and validate employee selection procedures. In addition, appraisal schemes can be devised to help employees identify the skills needed to perform current and potential jobs, and thereby form the basis for individual development at work.

Appraisal depends on the establishment of adequate measures of job performance on which judgements about effectiveness can be made. Criteria could include behaviours like 'is always on time', personality traits like 'ambitious', or outputs like 'sales volume'. Once criteria are settled upon, the scale of what is acceptable and unacceptable performance also needs to be defined. For example, it might be necessary to establish how many sales constitutes average, good or excellent job performance, and what is the minimum level necessary to be acceptable. Clearly, job appraisal criteria depend in part on adequate job analysis. The criteria should be relevant to the job at hand, and ideally other factors should not affect performance judgements. For example, 'dress and appearance' could be considered central to the job of a receptionist, but not a garage mechanic. Equally, all relevant criteria for job success should be considered for inclusion in the appraisal scheme if possible. If relevant factors are omitted then the criteria are said to be deficient. This can be serious for organisations because it is easy for perceptions about the fairness of the appraisal system to be influenced by a mismatch between appraisal criteria and job-relevant performance factors. Other structural factors affecting fairness are equality of opportunity to perform, and whether individual performance is influenced by co-workers.

Errors in appraisal can also be due to biases on the part of the appraiser, even if these are subconscious. Appraisals based on subjective assessments – for example, ratings of personality – rather than on performance outcomes can be subject to several sources of bias. Typical are the halo effect, one-sided ratings, central tendency, similarity to the rater and conflating dimensions. The halo effect is where the appraiser identifies a positive or negative aspect of an employee and bases his or her ratings on just that one aspect. One-sided ratings are where an appraiser may be unduly lenient or severe on all dimensions, for reasons not to do with performance. Central tendency is another form of one-sidedness, but in this case ratings are all average. Appraisers can also base their ratings on whether the employee is like, or similar to, them. Finally, conflating occurs if particular dimensions are wrongly linked, like absenteeism and lateness.

More pervasive aspects of bias can depend on characteristics of both appraisers and those being appraised. For example, older employees may be judged to be less effective than younger ones (Waldman and Avolio, 1986). Experienced raters have been found to be better at rating, as have employees who are high performers (Landy and Farr, 1980). A way to moderate biases is to use more than one appraiser, but in practice this can prove difficult.

Appraisal methods

Appraisal methods are ways of judging an employee's performance. Common approaches include ranking workers relative to each other, usually along one dimension. Ranking methods are easy to use, but they have a number of problems. Chief amongst these is that a ranking gives no idea of the level of performance achieved. For example, the top worker may make 200 washers an hour, the next highest 100, the third 98, and so on. Second, ranks do not indicate whether the performance achieved is effective because they do not relate to any performance criteria. A third problem is that the procedure becomes cumbersome with large numbers of workers. Checklists address some of these problems by providing a list of traits or behaviours that the appraiser can check as relevant to performance. However, simple checklists are all or none measures; for example, 'punctuality' is either ticked or not. Another disadvantage is that the checklist fails to distinguish between different job behaviours: they are all treated as of equal importance. This can be overcome by using weighted checklists, so that, for example, 'punctuality' might be rated on a 20-point scale and 'production rate' on a 100-point scale. This has the further benefit of making the appraiser and worker aware of the relative importance of the various facets of the job.

Rating scales involve the appraiser assessing performance scales that, for example, can range from 'all of the time' to 'never'. Thus some of the disadvantages of simple checklists can be avoided. Scales can be linked to behavioural descriptions at different levels. For example, when 'mixed standard rating scales' (Blanz and Ghiselli, 1972) are used, critical incidents of good, average and poor performance are put into statements on the appraisal form and raters indicate whether the worker exceeds, equals or falls below the standard.

A different way of appraising is to use **management by objectives** (MBO) (Drucker, 1954). Performance outcomes or objectives and the dates by which they are to be achieved are set. Action plans by which the objectives will be realised can also be outlined. In principle MBO can be imposed on employees or objectives and plans can be arrived at in discussion and negotiation with employees. Some research suggests that MBO is better suited to participative management styles (McConkey, 1983). The advantage of this method of appraisal is that managers and employees know what is expected of them. A disadvantage is that outcomes may not be wholly under the control of the employee.

Management by objectives has been adopted in a wide range of organisational settings. It describes a system of management which tries to relate organisational goals to the performance of individual workers. It involves the setting of objectives and targets, participation by individual managers in agreeing their objectives and the criteria for performance, and the review and appraisal of results. MBO means that subordinates need not be told exactly how to do their jobs, but instead they agree to, and are given, a set of tasks to do and results to achieve. Within agreed limits and the policies of the organisation, subordinates can be given the freedom to decide how to meet their objectives. Performance is measured in terms of accomplishment, rather than the ability to follow detailed instructions. To be effective, therefore, MBO is best suited to a participative management ethos rather than a style of management based on direction and control. MBO can be, and is, also used to motivate workers by linking performance to a system of rewards and career progression which recognises individual levels of contribution to organisational goals.

MBO has several attractive features, and some disadvantages. The advantages usually claimed for it include the following:

- it focuses attention on key areas where the organisation needs to be effective;
- it identifies problems in progress towards achieving objectives;
- it clarifies responsibilities and aids co-ordination of activities;
- it helps identify training needs;
- it helps provide a more equitable appraisal system;
- it improves communication between different levels in the organisation;
- it helps motivate individual workers.

Its drawbacks include the following:

- it has a strong focus on individual, rather than team, performance;
- it can be misused to impose targets on staff;
- some jobs are hard to define in terms of objectives, especially those such as counselling employees for which it is difficult to establish performance criteria;

- it is difficult to apply when organisational objectives are rapidly changing.

Several factors can be important in a successful MBO system. These include the commitment and support of top management; careful setting of key objectives and performance standards so that they are fair across individuals; objectives which are clearly defined, realistically attainable and measurable; and participation by staff in agreeing objectives.

Motivation at work

Working smarter, not harder, was mentioned at the beginning of the chapter as what distinguished 'superworkers' from others. In terms of operating new technology the need to utilise mental skills is apparent. However, that does not mean that the motivation to work at one's job is not an issue for organisations and employees. Motivation can be defined as a force which causes people to act; which directs behaviour to the attainment of specific goals; and which sustains the effort required in reaching those goals (Steers and Porter, 1983). Taylor held that workers were motivated by material gain and money. Since his time theorists have suggested that individual needs are important, or that the costs and benefits of work are judged in a rational way, or that a wide conception of rewards is critical.

Maslow's need hierarchy

One of the best-known need theories is that of Maslow (1965, 1970). In essence the theory states that motivation is a function of needs which can be ordered into five categories:

- physiological needs such as food, water, sleep and sex;
- safety needs such as the need for shelter and physical well-being;
- social needs such as the need to be accepted by others, and the need for love, affection and friendship;

- esteem needs such as the need to be recognised for achievements, to be admired and respected;
- self-actualisation needs such as the need to attain a sense of fulfilment.

Maslow suggested that the lower-order needs had to be met before a person could move to the higher-order ones. As needs are met they no longer act as motivators and so the dominant motivator is to be found at the next level. In the world of work a salary meets survival and safety needs, and social interaction with fellow workers satisfies some social needs. Making a success at work can meet esteem and self-actualisation needs. The effect of Maslow's need hierarchy has been to delineate potential needs beyond basic ones, and thus focus consideration on non-monetary incentives to motivate workers.

McClelland's 'need for achievement' theory

Maslow's hierarchy of needs was not developed specifically for the work context. McClelland (1961, 1975), on the other hand, proposed three needs central to work motivation which are encompassed by his achievement motivation theory. The three needs are need for achievement, for example to get the job done, and succeed; need for power, for example to control others and have influence; and the need for affiliation, for example to be liked and accepted by work colleagues. Workers are supposed to have a mixture of these needs, which may vary from person to person. However, one or more may be dominant. To assess a person's motivational needs McClelland used a version of the thematic apperception test (TAT). This test involves the person's studying ambiguous pictures for a short time and then writing the story the pictures suggest to them. The stories are then scored in a standard way to obtain a motivational profile of the person. Like any projective procedure the TAT is open to criticism concerning how it is scored, because different scorers can interpret the stories differently. Research into worker motivation suggests that those with a high need for achievement do attain personal success in their jobs, provided the type of work they do promotes personal achievement. An example would be where there is a direct relation between individual effort and job outcomes like salespeople working on commission. The theory has led to programmes to improve worker motivation in the workplace by matching profiles with jobs to allow individuals to realise their dominant needs (McClelland, 1988).

In contrast to need theories which focus on the individual, other motivational theories concentrate on the nature and structure of jobs as instrumental in motivating workers. Foremost amongst these are Herzberg's two-factor theory and the job characteristics model.

Herzberg's two-factor theory

The two-factor theory developed by Herzberg (1966) is concerned with the factors which affect job satisfaction, rather than motivation directly. The theory asserts that job satisfaction is the result of the presence of certain job aspects. These are responsibility, achievement, recognition, job content, advancement and personal growth. These aspects he called 'motivators'. In contrast, aspects whose absence results in job dissatisfaction he called 'hygienes', and comprise company policy and administration, supervision, interpersonal relations, working conditions and salary. The theory emerged from the analysis of the survey responses of white-collar, professional workers. Motivators relate to job content, and hygiene factors relate to job context. Subsequent research has not confirmed the presence of two distinct factors (Schneider and Locke, 1971), and others have suggested that the theory applies more to white-collar workers than other groups.

Herzberg's theory helped to introduce strategies of 'job enrichment' designed to increase worker motivation. These programmes involved redesigning jobs to give more responsibility in planning, execution and evaluating to workers. Job enrichment programmes have been implemented in a number of European and US companies, but their success has been difficult to determine because of methodological problems. Typically, large numbers of jobs are altered at the same time in any one situation, making rigorous comparisons impossible (Miner, 1983).

Job characteristics model

The job characteristics model (JCM) proposed by Hackman and Oldham (1976) suggests that worker motivation is affected by whether workers perceive their jobs as meaningful, whether they have a sense of responsibility in the job, and whether they have some knowledge of the results of their work. These perceptions are the result of five core job characteristics, which are:

1   Skill variety – the extent to which a job demands a diversity of skills and abilities, and hence is perceived as meaningful;
2   task identity – whether a job is seen as a coherent whole with an identifiable outcome which the worker can relate to his or her work effort;
3   task significance – the degree to which the job impacts on others in the company or its customers;
4   autonomy – the amount of latitude the worker has to carry out the job; and
5   feedback – whether the job allows the worker to get direct information on performance effectiveness.

The theory asserts that skill variety, task identity and task significance affect the perception of job meaningfulness, autonomy affects the perception of responsibility associated with the job, and feedback affects the experience of work outcomes.

Motivation depends on the three perceptions. However, these can be moderated by other variables such as 'growth need strength'. Those low in growth need will not be motivated by increases in the five job characteristics, whereas those high in growth need will benefit. Research has tended to support the job characteristics view of worker motivation (Fried and Ferris, 1987). There are strong links between the job characteristics model and theories of job design and redesign (see Chapter 2).

Equity theory of motivation

In contrast to need theories, several alternative accounts stress the rational, logical element in workers. The equity theory of motivation is one of the latter. In essence the theory suggests that workers conduct a cost–benefit analysis of their job (Adams, 1965). If the analysis results in the worker's perceiving that he or she is being treated fairly then motivation will be maintained. The cost–benefit analysis is calculated on 'inputs' such as worker experience, education and qualifications; 'outcomes' such as pay, perks, recognition and challenging work; and 'comparison to others', such as co-workers, similar jobs, or other work experience. Demotivation is one of the results of 'underpayment inequity', where workers perceive that the outcomes they receive are too low in relation to inputs. Interestingly, the theory suggests that workers can take several actions in the 'underpayment' context. One that follows demotivation is reducing the amount of input to the job, another is to try to increase outcomes, a third is to change the comparison by comparing themselves with different people, and the fourth is quitting the job. Where outcomes are perceived to exceed inputs in comparison with others, an 'overpayment inequity' is created. The possibilities here are to decrease outcomes, increase inputs, change the comparison group or job, or distort the situation by, for example, imagining that one's work is of higher quality than one's peers'. Research has shown that equity theory has potential as an explanation of worker motivation, and that individuals differ in their sensitivity to inequities. For example, giving workers a higher-status job title can lead to increased inputs without any increase in pay (Greenberg and Ornstein, 1983).

Expectancy or VIE theory

VIE stands for valence, instrumentality and expectancy and is associated with Vroom (1964). The theory is concerned with the rational costs and benefits workers associate with their jobs. Benefits include things like recognition and job satisfaction, and costs encompass reprimands and sackings. Motivation is the result of a combination of valence, which is the desirability of an outcome to the worker, instrumentality, which is the perceived likelihood of an outcome given a particular work behaviour, and expectancy, which is perceived connection between the worker's effort and performance.

It is clear that many of the theories of motivation outlined above include similar ideas about what are important motivators at work. Rewards, recognition and responsibility appear constant components in the theories discussed. Where need theories differ from rational theories is in how the components have their influence on workers. In the former needs must be satisfied, in the latter a rational weighing of pros and cons must be perceived as positive.

Summary

This chapter has considered the main personnel functions related to the demands of new technology. The aim of the personnel functions is to match people to tasks and jobs. Prime amongst the demands made is the need to learn to use computer-controlled technology. The skills required are more mental than manual, and thus a premium is placed on cognitive skill acquisition and training of mental skills and problem-solving techniques. New technology has not altered the basic personnel function at one level: organisations still need to recruit, appraise and motivate people for the jobs they are required to do. Thus the basic aspects of personnel work have been outlined, and related to the changing requirements of work resulting from technology where relevant.

Chapter 4

Mental work

■ Human factors   66

■ Mental work and technology   68
Workload measures   73

■ Variability in mental performance   76
Work environment and performance   76
Illumination   77
Temperature   77
Noise   78
Individual states and mental
  performance   80
Changes in performance with time
  of day   84
Shiftwork   85
Latent performance deficits   86

■ Task allocation   88

■ Summary   90

THIS CHAPTER IS CONCERNED with demands made by complex, often computer-based, technologies, and in particular the way in which modern technology has increased the emphasis on mental, rather than physical, work. Interest centres on mental work and processing and the relationship it has to the design of equipment, the workplace and work tasks.

Technological processes have become very complex in many economic sectors, for example aviation, power generation, chemical production, transport, manufacturing, and service industries such as banking and commodity transactions. A feature of the changing methods in these sectors is that they rely on computers for information and control.

Key questions which arise are centred round how individuals cope with computerised information and control. For example, what are the limitations in mental capacity and their effect in dealing with information? How should functions be allocated between the technology and the person, and what are the psychological effects of the choice? How does mental performance change under the influence of environmental stressors such as noise, and at different times of day and night?

Human factors

Traditionally, human factors, and ergonomics, have concerned themselves with the physical working environment and how people behave as components of the human–machine system. They have been concerned with the design of seating, knobs and dials, lighting, and heat and noise effects on performance, to name a few. Interest in human factors has remained high with the advent of computerisation in the workplace, because more and more people are required to operate sophisticated systems through computer control or support. The field, along with cognitive ergonomics, has become much more concerned with people as a cognitive part of the system; that is, with how people process information from, think about, control and react to the systems they are engaged with. A consequence is that system designers have the opportunity to consider the relative strengths and weaknesses of humans and machines, and what functions should be performed by each. Machine operators, for example, are adaptable, can handle unexpected events, can think, can learn from mistakes, can get tired and stressed, and react differently in hot or noisy conditions. Machines, on the other hand, do not get tired, can handle routine and automated functions easily, and are less affected by variations in temperature and noise.

Human factors research has thrown up some general principles concerning displays, controls and the working environment. These are far too extensive to detail here, but a summary of some recommendations will convey the types of outcomes traditionally dealt with. The most common displays used to transmit information are visual and auditory, although smell is also used, for example in natural gas to warn of a leak. Visual displays are good for conveying complex information, and can carry several messages at once. Auditory displays often serve an alarm function, and are good for urgent messages. Controls, for example switches, knobs, buttons, levers, etc., should be compatible with the operators' physical dimensions, should mirror the machine actions they produce, should be clearly marked, adequately spaced and arranged to avoid unintentional use, should be easily discriminable from one another, and standardised if possible. Workspaces should be designed with performance efficiency, operator comfort, safety, operator limitations and machine design in mind. Sanders and McCormick (1987) propose that important functions and operations should be able to take place in a central location relative to the operator, so for example relevant displays should be in front of the operator. Machines which are most frequently used should be conveniently located; machine components (displays and controls) should be grouped according to function, and placed in order of sequence of use. The workplace should take into account the physical dimensions of workers; for example, seats should be designed for comfort.

Mental work and technology

Complex technologies entail their operators in handling considerable amounts of information. The system displays the information to the operator, who needs to perceive it, remember some or all of it, make decisions on the basis of it, and then act to control the system. For example, the number of controls and displays in power station control rooms increased dramatically between the 1950s and 1970s, from under 500 to more than 3000 in 1975. Now many control rooms in nuclear power stations, chemical production installations and the like utilise computer displays. Aircraft cockpits initially contained very little information, but since the Second World War commercial aircraft cockpits have had large numbers of displays. Recently computers have replaced dials and other more traditional displays, and the pilot can call up information about the state of the aircraft on 'head-up displays' (HUDs). In power stations controls and displays have been replaced by computer keyboards and screens.

The main framework for trying to understand how people handle the mental processes involved in dealing with vast amounts of information is the **information processing approach**. This was developed in the late 1940s and 1950s, and has become the dominant way of thinking about how sensory information is perceived, transformed and utilised by the mind as the basis for actions. Typically the approach is concerned with the way information is handled by the mind – for example, how fast it is transformed and how accurately, what mental operations are necessary to allow appropriate actions to be taken, and with the general nature of mental representations – rather than with the contents of the mind *per se*, although these are of course important. More recent developments have tended to redress this balance and place emphasis on the understandings an operator has when dealing with complex technology and processes.

Human factors have been concerned with how systems and machines can be designed taking account of the limitations in human information processing. One of the key limitations has been the capacity of the mind in handling information. The issue is usually discussed under the rubric of mental workload, because notions about how mentally demanding a task is, and how much mental capacity is available to meet those demands, are intimately related.

An aviation example serves to illustrate the importance of understanding mental workload. The aviation industry is heavily regulated so that safety receives considerable attention. In the UK the Civil Aviation Authority (CAA) is involved in regulation. In the USA the Federal Aviation Administration governs similar aspects. One of the design considerations for aircraft makers is how many people – pilots, co-pilots, navigators and flight engineers – should crew the aircraft. Clearly, the higher the number, the higher the cost to operating companies in flying the aircraft. One of the purposes of technology which automates some of the activities carried out by people is to remove the need for the person. Several years ago many aircraft required three crew on the flight deck. Nowadays the number is much more likely to be two. Obviously the reduction in numbers means that there may be more to do per individual crew member for the two crew as compared to the previous three. Of course new technology can carry out some of the tasks previously done by the crew, but the question remains as to what can reasonably be allocated to fewer crew.

Federal Aviation Regulation (FAR) 25 specifies the general constraints on the designer's freedom to allocate work to pilots and other crew: 'Each pilot compartment and its equipment must allow the minimum flight crew to perform their duties without unreasonable concentration and fatigue' and 'Minimum flight crew must be established ... for safe operation ... considering ... the workload on individual crew members' (cited in Kantowitz and Caspar, 1988). FAR25 goes on to detail workload factors relevant to cockpit design:

1   The accessibility, ease, and simplicity of operation of all necessary flight, power, and equipment controls ...

2   The accessibility and conspicuity of all necessary instruments and failure warning devices . . .

3   The number, urgency, and complexity of operating procedures . . .

There are two broad approaches to mental workload: theoretical and practical. Theoretical analysis is founded on laboratory investigations into the mechanisms of attention and working memory and performance, in this case perceptual–motor, cognitive and memory performance. Performance in this case is not simple reflex reactions, but sequences of actions. Practical approaches rely on subjective and physiological responses to task difficulty.

A key assumption underlying theoretical approaches is that there is a mental capacity for handling information and making decisions about it which is involved in all task activity. Therefore if the task becomes more difficult, or you are asked to do more than one thing at a time, mental capacity will stretch only so far before becoming overloaded. Once the capacity limit has been reached, performance starts to break down by becoming less accurate and fluent, or by becoming slower. An important point, therefore, is that mental workload is not simply a question of task difficulty, but is a function of the amount of demand on mental resources in relation to the amount of mental resources, or mental capacity, available.

Two broad theoretical ideas entail the assumption of a general-purpose limited capacity. The first invokes the notion of a single-channel processor (Broadbent, 1958). The second views attention as a pool of resource or energy which is available for mental activity (Kahneman, 1973). The single channel entails the idea of capacity as the ability to process so much information per unit time. The attentional resource idea implies having an amount of attention to devote to one or more tasks. In other words, one framework considers 'throughput' of information, the other sees capacity as being like an energy source or mental battery. Thus you can be asked either to work too quickly, or to do too much for your capacity to cope with. Not all commentators see capacity and resources as equivalent metaphors. Wickens (1992) distinguishes capacity as an upper limit on information processing rate, and resources as being applied to processing within that limit. The idea, then, is that increasing mental resources can be applied to a task, increasing performance thereby, until an upper limit on performance is reached. Thereafter further resources will not improve performance.

The concept of limited capacity suggests that when capacity is overloaded, performance will suffer. Studies in the laboratory which ask people to do two things at once (the dual task paradigm) show that, in general, performance on any one of the tasks is not as good as when doing that task on its own. This finding lends support to the idea that there is indeed a general-purpose capacity limit. However, that is not the end of the story because research has also shown that the amount of interference in performance between two tasks depends on the nature of the tasks. Tasks that are similar to each other interfere more with each other than do tasks which are dissimilar. The most documented dimensions of similarity are whether a task utilises the same input modality (e.g. auditory or visual), the same central processing (e.g. language or vision), or the same output modality (e.g. verbal or manual).

Observations of differential interference effects as a function of task similarity have led theorists to suggest that instead of a general-purpose limited capacity, it would be sensible to think in terms of several different sources of mental resource. Where a task draws on the same resource then the possibility of overload is increased compared to the case where a task places demands on different mental resources. Hockey (1996) makes the point that workload, therefore, implies 'a concern with the overloading of capacity within a particular resource, or set of resources'. He also points out that there are practical consequences to considering mental work as potentially drawing on the same or several different mental resources. Task interference may be the result of poor work design, but in the case of overloading a particular resource the overall level of concentration of work demand, or the rate of work, should be reduced, whereas in the case where two different resources could be used, one stream of information should be presented visually rather than both in the auditory mode, or the equipment design could be altered to allow manual and voice outputs.

Many commentators conceptualise work demands in terms of the drain on mental resources. However, the other view, presented above, was that capacity should be seen as a limit in information processing. In the 1950s, when the idea of a single-channel information processor gained popularity, the notion of information carried quite specific connotations. In particular, information was considered in terms of decision-making: the more choices between possible alternatives, the longer it took to make a response (Hick, 1952). Information from the environment or task, and the length of time it took to process and respond to it, was linked to how probable the event was (Hyman, 1953). Probable, or likely, events carried less information, and hence demanded less of the limited-capacity central processor. The consequences of this view are that very familiar tasks and environments are less mentally demanding because they are more predictable. This conceptualisation has been used to explain at least some of the findings from the dual task paradigm (Broadbent, 1982).

Clearly this has practical implications for work design and the use of technology. One implication is that to minimise workload, control sequences ideally should be standardised so that the conditions that give rise to them, and the series of responses necessary, are always the same. A second implication is that training, and so familiarisation with a task and equipment, will help to reduce mental workload. It is often the case that successful dual task performance has depended on considerable practice, and/or high levels of existing skill gained through considerable experience (Allport et al., 1972).

In terms of the resources point of view, becoming skilled at a task through practice is considered to demand less by way of resources. The processing was thought to become 'automatic' in the sense of requiring little mental effort to carry out, and being initiated without conscious, or effortful, control.

The foregoing discussion illustrates the need to distinguish the kind of performance demanded by a set of tasks. Is the requirement for skilled and practised performance, or for novel activity, and what kind of cognitive control is required, effortful or not? Rasmussen (e.g. 1986) has proposed a taxonomy of task activity: skill-, rule- and knowledge-based activity. Familiarisation and practice allow the use of skill- and rule-based activity. New situations and tasks require knowledge-based activity. Skill-based control is where learned responses are produced by appropriate conditions, rather like the automatic processing mentioned above. Rule-based control is where learned rules are applied in familiar situations in order to achieve specified goals. Knowledge-based control is akin to problem-solving, and is needed in unfamiliar situations. Knowledge-based activity is considered to be highly effortful, whereas skill-based activity demands relatively little mental effort. Chapter 5 outlines how this perspective has been applied to the analysis of human error, and its relationship to some of the world's major catastrophes such as the near nuclear meltdown at Three Mile Island in Pennsylvania.

Workload measures

There are three measurement approaches that have been used in connection with mental workload: behavioural, subjective and physiological. Current approaches to measuring mental workload emphasise a transactional perspective: workload is a function of both task and individual characteristics, such as task difficulty, skill level, effort capacity and motivational level. All workload measures can be considered for their suitability in a given situation by comparing them against several criteria. The criteria include sensitivity, diagnosticity, intrusiveness and ease of use. Sensitivity refers to the responsiveness of a measure to changes in mental workload. Diagnosticity refers to the extent that a measure identifies the particular mental resources involved. Intrusiveness refers to whether the measure interferes with the task being assessed. Finally, ease of use is concerned with how straightforward the measure is to administer. For example, physiological measures are not very easy to use because they use specialist equipment and involve placing electrodes on a person, and the administrator usually requires training to use the measure reliably.

The theoretical approach derived from studies of attention and dual task performance gives rise to behavioural methods for measuring workload, in terms of attempting to determine the amount of mental capacity required by a task. The methods can be divided into primary and secondary task measures.

Primary task performance measures are a direct means of assessing the impact of demands. For example, as a task gets more difficult, or the person gets tired, it is reasonable to expect more errors or for the task to take longer. However, primary task performance measures on their own are not usually sufficient to measure mental workload. The reason is that performance levels can often be maintained, or protected, in the face of increased demands or fatigue. Craig and Cooper (1992), in reviewing studies of fatigue, sleep loss and performance, concluded that direct indices of performance on continuous **perceptual–motor tasks**, such as speed of response, frequently showed no decrement during prolonged task activity. The situation is complicated, though, because what constitutes acceptable performance needs to be defined and clarified for a task. The importance of this point is illustrated by Chmiel *et al.* (1995), who showed that even after the loss of a whole night's sleep, and after several hours of work on a computerised adaptive control task, performance quality targets could still be achieved, but at a cost of working more slowly. In short, different aspects of performance may be traded off against each other, and this aspect may be missed if primary task performance measures do not measure the important aspects of performance. Even if these considerations are addressed by primary measures, they may not pick up differences in mental workload between two tasks because the differences may be hidden by having spare mental capacity.

Secondary task techniques attempt to provide an indication of mental demand from the primary task in terms of spare capacity.

One way of examining spare capacity is to add a standardised secondary task to the primary task, and instruct the operator to respond to the secondary task only when the primary task allows it. Demands of different primary tasks can then be compared by measuring performance on the secondary task. The more demanding a primary task, the less spare capacity available for the secondary task, and so the worse the performance on the secondary task.

Subjective workload measures are not theoretically grounded, but rather are a practical alternative to behavioural measures. In the field they have the advantages of low intrusiveness and ease of use. The technique, in essence, asks operators to report on how hard they think they are working. Thus a single rating scale of, for example, mental effort or task difficulty may be used. An example is the Cooper–Harper scale, developed for the aviation context, and its modifications designed to make it more generally applicable. Operators are asked to make a series of yes–no decisions to a series of questions, such as 'Are errors small and inconsequential?' If the answer is no, then operators are asked how much mental effort is required to control errors. The answers are converted to a ten-point scale where 1 represents minimal mental effort. Other, recent, measures, developed mainly within aviation contexts, have considered multidimensional aspects of rating mental workload. The subjective workload assessment test (SWAT) asks for subjective ratings of demands on time, mental effort and feelings of stress, using three-point scales. The NASA Task Load Index (NASA-TLX) has six scales: temporal demand; mental demand; mental effort; frustration level; physical demand; and performance. In both cases the scales are combined to give an overall measure of mental workload. Subjective measures show good sensitivity to changes in task demands, and are possibly the most widely used of workload measures.

Physiological measures, such as brain evoked potentials, pupil dilation, changes in hormonal levels and **heart rate variability**, have been used to index information-processing demands. Measuring brain electrical activity through the use of electrodes on the scalp is thought to pick up cognitive processing (Wickens,

1992). Tattersall and Hockey (1995), cited in Hockey (1996), have shown that heart rate variability decrease occurs in parallel with increased levels of processing demands. Pupil dilation has often been found to correlate well with increased demands in a variety of **cognitive tasks**. However, there are problems in interpreting physiological measures since changes in them can be due to changes in many other functions. Thus physiological indices related to task demands may reflect more general nervous system activity in response to mental demands. Hockey (1996) suggests they are best used with performance or subjective measures allowing inferences to be made about the effort needed to reach measured performance levels, and the relation between energy mobilisation and perceptions of mental demand.

Variability in mental performance

A strong interest is whether and how mental performance changes as a function of aspects of the environment, and changes in the individual. Examples of the former are noise, heat, incentives and other environmental stressors; and examples of the latter are fatigue, sleep loss, having a cold, and drinking coffee or alcohol.

Work environment and performance

Psychologists have long been interested in whether and how conditions at work affect work behaviour and productivity. In terms of task performance, interest has traditionally centred on perceptual–motor behaviour, reflecting the work interests of the time. More recently, more direct cognitive activity has been investigated in various tasks relevant to the use of new technology and computers. Those aspects which have tended to receive most consideration are fairly obvious: noise, heat and illumination. Some physical aspects of the environment are more prevalent in some jobs than others, and are more important to performance than others. In addition, environmental conditions affect different tasks differently.

Illumination

The level of lighting was manipulated in one of the classic series of studies in occupational psychology: those by Mayo at the Hawthorne plant of the Western Electrical Company. The researchers were interested in the connection between illumination and productivity. In their case they discovered the Hawthorne effect mentioned in Chapter 1, but subsequent investigation has demonstrated that performance improves with increasing light levels up to a point where it levels off. Where the point is depends on the type of task. For example, the recommended level of lighting for a hospital operating theatre is twenty to a hundred times that of a general office environment. Overlighting can produce problems too, such as distracting glare and visual fatigue.

Temperature

Extreme heat, or cold, is perceived as uncomfortable and in some cases debilitating. Temperatures lower than 0°C or higher than approximately 32°C have produced reductions in manual and mental performance (Kobrick and Fine, 1983). On the basis of a number of studies the United States National Institute for Occupational Safety and Health (NIOSH) produced guidelines in 1972 relating to heat limits in industry. The guidelines show the upper limits for unimpaired performance as a function of the thermal environment. In effect the function illustrates that performance can be maintained at a high temperature (greater than 40°C) if exposure time is brief. However, performance can be affected above about 30°C at exposure times exceeding about three hours. The limit for any combination of temperature and exposure duration is judged to be well below those for physiological tolerance in general.

Other studies have shown that the NIOSH guidelines are too general and that as temperature increases, and the duration of exposure to temperature increases, different mental tasks are affected differently. Ramsey and Morrissey (1978) showed that for cognitive and reaction time tasks, such as mental arithmetic, visual search and speeded classification, there was a trade-off between temperature and exposure duration, similar to the NIOSH limits, although marked impairments in performance were rare below about 35°C unless exposure times were greater than two and a half hours. In contrast, continuous performance tasks, such as tracking, vigilance and sustained attention, show an effect only of temperature, and not of exposure duration. These tasks are sensitive to temperatures above about 30°C, and impairment gets worse as temperature increases (see Hockey, 1986, for a review).

It is also the case that prolonged changes in the environment lead to acclimatisation, hence moderating the effects of temperature (Poulton, 1970). Other factors influence the perception of temperature and its effects. Thus increasing humidity leads to considerably increased feelings of discomfort for the same temperature of 26°C (Fanger, 1970).

Noise

In some occupations high levels of noise are an everyday part of working life. For example, printing presses, automatic looms and machine cutting tools all generate loud noise. The effects of noise on performance have turned out to be quite complex. For example, in the USA the Environment Protection Agency concluded in 1974 that noise did not generally impair performance unless it exceeded 90 decibels; that intermittent or unpredictable noise was more disruptive than continuous noise; that high-frequency (high-pitched) noise was more disruptive than low-frequency noise; and that noise was more likely to lead to higher work error than to lowered rates of performance. Indeed, Kerr (1950) showed that mean noise level at work was the most potent predictor of accident frequency, although not severity.

Hockey (1986) suggests that the effects of intermittent noise can be related to its startling consequences, and the effect on performance produced by sudden noise can be thought of as 'being due to distraction'.

Continuous loud noise of many frequencies (broad-band noise) has been shown to have both positive and negative effects on different types of task. Impairments in performance have been found in sustained-attention (vigilance, i.e. watching for something – a signal – to occur) tasks under some conditions, but not others. The conditions likely to produce impairment are when signals are difficult to detect, and when the task situation encourages risky decision behaviour (Broadbent, 1979). Where multiple sources of information need to be monitored the effects of noise appear more readily. For example, monitoring a bank of 20 dials for a needle to go into the danger zone is affected by noise. Broadbent (1954) found an increase in the number of slow detection responses with 100 decibels of noise.

Hockey (1970) asked people to carry out a central pursuit tracking task at the same time as monitoring six lights arranged around it for infrequent flashes. Hockey observed that the normal decrement in performance on pursuit tracking was prevented by noise over the 40 minutes of the test, but that detection rates were higher for the two central lights than for the four lights in the more extreme locations. He interpreted this result as being due to an increase in the selectivity of attention in noise.

In tasks where people are asked to respond continuously, for example to whichever of five lights comes on next (**serial responding**), the main effect of noise is to promote an increase in the speed of responding or a decrease in accuracy. Sometimes both speed and accuracy are affected. The effects of noise on the task increase with the time spent doing the task.

In terms of a more cognitive task, Hamilton *et al.* (1977) showed that problem-solving was affected by noise depending on whether working memory was involved. As memory load increased, problem-solving time increased in noise, compared to a decrease in time if people were offered a monetary incentive.

Some studies have also shown that there are effects of noise even after the noise has stopped. Twenty to thirty minutes' exposure to noise impairs subsequent performance in quiet conditions, on problem-solving tasks, perceptual classification and serial reaction.

In addition, noise potentially impairs communication at work, and the ability to use acoustic cues as feedback from machines. Noise can also be perceived as uncomfortable, and at high levels can lead to physical damage to the ear.

One aspect of noise that has become more prominent with the advent of open-plan offices is the effect, not of broad-band noise, but of irrelevant speech on performance. The influence of irrelevant speech is especially pertinent to many workplaces using computer technology, since very often the technology is sited in open-plan environments. Summarising recent research, Smith (1995) concludes that irrelevant speech affects aspects of memory performance for verbal materials (ordered recall), that the effect of irrelevant speech is independent of its intensity (within the range 55–95 decibels), that the meaning of the speech is unimportant, and that the effect seems to be on memory rather than perception. Vocal music has been found to have a greater disruptive effect than instrumental music.

Individual states and mental performance

In addition to their interest in whether aspects of the working environment produce changes in performance, psychologists have also been interested in whether variability in mental performance can be a function of changes within the individual. Studies have focused on changes to an individual's state that appear most common: for example, changes due to fatigue, sleep loss, colds and flu, alcohol, caffeine (in coffee and tea), and taking food, especially lunch.

Fatigue

Fatigue can be defined as 'weariness from task activity over time' (Craig and Cooper, 1992). It is important to consider whether there are any effects of fatigue during a task, and also following a task. Surprisingly, it has proved quite difficult to demonstrate direct effects of fatigue. Often no effect is found on perceptual–motor tasks, although some studies have shown that performance becomes less accurate. However, on continuous serial reaction, carried out for half an hour, slow responses increase, even though overall response rate is not affected. Thus response variability increases with fatigue. Errors were found to occur near the slow responses. These findings have led to the suggestion that the mental system has micro-sleeps when fatigued, leading to slow responses and errors. In terms of a more cognitive, adaptive control, task, Chmiel *et al.* (1995) have shown that fatigue has little effect, even after several hours of doing the same task. Only when fatigue was combined with lack of sleep was performance impaired.

The picture of fatigue changes somewhat when studies of skilled, integrated and relatively complex performance are considered. A famous series of studies using a flight simulator, carried out by Bartlett and colleagues in the 1940s in Cambridge, UK, illustrates fatigue effects on the integrity of performance. The task was to fly a course in the simulator whilst monitoring various pieces of equipment, for example the fuel gauge. The task often lasted four hours or so (mimicking the flight times for wartime raids over the Continent from Britain). Bartlett found that aircraft control and timing manoeuvres deteriorated; tolerance to fluctuations, for example in bearing and airspeed, increased; memory lapses, inattentiveness and unforced errors increased; the integrity of the task declined, so that subtasks such as monitoring the fuel gauge and holding a course became more independent of each other; irritability and awareness of discomfort (e.g. the hardness of the cockpit seat) rose; and the effects were modulated by pilots' awareness that they were near the end of the task.

Broadbent (1979) noted that it was very difficult to find a test which demonstrated fatigue following a task. The reasons may be due to the fact that fatigue tests were of short duration, and potentially momentarily arousing due possibly to their novelty value. There is some evidence that, given a choice, people will choose strategies for performing a task which require less mental effort when fatigued, even if the strategy is less likely to lead to success (Holding, 1983). The latter observation has led to the suggestion that fatigue be defined as an 'aversion to effort', and this definition has quite wide acceptance.

Sleep loss

Young adults of working age sleep for roughly seven and a half hours a night, with surprisingly little variation. Older adults tend to sleep slightly less long. Sleep loss can be categorised as total, partial and selective. Total sleep loss is a night or more without sleep; partial sleep loss is some number of hours below normal, for a night or more; and selective loss is where either REM (rapid eye movement) or slow-wave sleep is disrupted. REM sleep primarily occurs later in the sleep cycle, whereas slow-wave sleep primarily occurs early. Therefore 'staying up late' tends to disrupt slow-wave sleep, whereas 'waking early' tends to disrupt REM sleep. If people are woken from REM sleep they tend to report the fact that they were dreaming. Slow-wave sleep is deep sleep where the dominant frequency in brain electrical activity, measured by **EEG recording**, decreases, and is of a higher voltage.

In general the effects of sleep loss are more likely to occur after some time has been spent working on a task. Impaired performance has been found on continuous tasks such as serial reaction, and on **working memory** tasks (see Hockey, 1986, and Craig and Cooper, 1992, for reviews). Williams *et al.* (1959) found deterioration on a number of performance measures over four days of sleep deprivation. One effect was to increase the variability in responding. The fastest responses remained much the same over the sleep loss period, but the number of slow responses increased, and they also got slower. This result and others suggest that going without sleep produces brief periods of processing inefficiency, or micro-sleeps, in otherwise normal functioning. However, Hockey (1970b, cited in Hockey, 1986) studied the effects of 30 hours of sleep loss on the dual tracking and monitoring task mentioned in the section on noise. He found that sleep loss affected the tracking task most, and that the normally large differences in monitoring reaction time between central and extreme light positions were reduced. He interpreted these findings as showing a reduction of selectivity in attention when sleep-deprived, the opposite of the effect found for noise. Interesting tasks tend to counteract the effects of sleep loss.

Colds and flu

Smith (1995) reports that influenza infection, but not cold virus infection, increased reaction time on tasks where there was uncertainty about when to respond, and about where the stimulus to respond to would appear. In contrast, colds impaired a tracking task whereas flu did not. Neither colds nor flu appeared to impair performance on complex cognitive tasks such as logical reasoning. Thus the effects of colds and flu seem limited to perceptual–motor tasks. Smith also notes that in terms of performance, people with colds were more sensitive to the effects of alcohol and noise.

Alcohol

Studies of performance involving large doses of alcohol have led to the observations that it impairs tracking, increases body sway, reduces memory performance, slows decision-making and can leave residual impairments which can last for at least 14 hours (Smith, 1995).

Caffeine

Quite large doses of caffeine, over 200 mg or the equivalent of a mug of real coffee, have been shown to improve performance on a variety of tasks. For example, caffeine may increase psychomotor speed, reduce simple and choice reaction times, improve the ability to maintain attention, increase the speed of retrieving facts from general knowledge, and increase the speed of logical reasoning. Memory tasks not dependent on speed have been shown to be relatively unaffected. It is not clear whether lower doses (equivalent to a cup of tea, or instant coffee) have the same effect (see Smith, 1995).

Food

'Post-lunch dip' has entered common language to describe the feeling of lethargy following the meal in the middle of the day. Research has shown there is indeed a decrease in alertness and sustained attention after having eaten lunch. Smith and colleagues (see Smith, 1995) have shown that the size of the dip in performance depends on the type of task and the nature of the meal, amongst other things. Meal size influences the frequency of lapses of attention. High-protein meals have led to increased distractibility, whereas high-carbohydrate meals have been shown to slow reactions to stimuli in the periphery. Thus the kind of nutrients in the meal appear to change the way attention is affected. Post-lunch dip can be reduced by taking caffeine after the meal, or by increasing alertness through exposure to noise.

Smith (1995) also reports that breakfast has no effect on attention, but does influence memory and reasoning. Recall of word lists improved after subjects had had breakfast, compared to having no breakfast, whereas logical reasoning was impaired. The evening meal, in contrast, was shown to improve performance on a logical reasoning task, but no effects were found on sustained attention or recall and recognition memory tasks.

Changes in performance with time of day

It is now well known that certain bodily functions vary over time. Examples are biorhythms, and the menstrual cycle in women, which cycle over periods of about 28 or so days. Of particular interest in the present context are changes which vary over the course of a day. These are called **circadian rhythms**. Probably the best known is the body temperature rhythm. Body temperature rises from about 8 a.m. throughout the day until it reaches a peak in the evening, whereupon it declines until it reaches a nadir or low point in the small hours of the morning, between about 3 and 7 a.m. Subjective alertness follows a similar pattern, and most people are happiest sleeping at night and being awake during the day.

A question for psychologists, therefore, is whether mental performance shows effects of time of day. In general, research has shown that perceptual–motor and more cognitive task performance does vary through the day. Folkard (1983) showed that between the hours of 8 a.m. to 8 p.m. simple serial search speed increased, whereas working memory speed increased in the morning, but then declined. Immediate memory retention decreased over the whole period. Over the whole 24 hours it has been shown that performance on a low memory load task follows the rhythm for body temperature, whereas performance on a high memory load task is out of phase; that is, when temperature is low performance is high and vice versa.

Smith (1995) concludes from a number of studies that performance changes over a day could be as much as plus or minus 15 per cent of the daily average. He summarises as follows: tasks involving immediate memory are performed best in the early morning; working memory tasks are performed best in the middle of the day; retrieval from semantic memory is quicker later in the day; selective attention changes over the day, with selectivity getting less as the day goes on; time of day effects in sustained attention are small, excepting the post-lunch dip; and that perceptual–motor tasks are performed more quickly, but less accurately, later in the day.

Shiftwork

Many advanced societies have gradually evolved to the point where 24-hour working is a significant part of the economy. Folkard (1996) reports that **shiftwork** varies with the size and nature of the organisation: there is twice as much shiftwork in organisations employing more than 50 employees, and there is more shiftwork in transport and communications (40 per cent) than in building and engineering (5 per cent).

Changes in performance depending on the shift have been observed. Folkard and Monk (1979) summarise several studies of job performance where continuous measures of speed or accuracy have been obtained. These show a rhythmical change with a low point for performance around 3 a.m. Interestingly there is also a dip around and shortly after midday, probably reflecting 'post-lunch dip'. The rhythmical effects are thought to be due to two principal types of causes: those due to time of day, and those due to sleep disruption and loss.

A key observation from studies of shiftworking is that workers on shifts suffer disruption to the normal sleep pattern, leading to sleep loss. Duration of sleep is a function of the time during the day or night at which a person goes to sleep. Going to sleep between about 9 p.m. and 1 a.m. leads to a normal amount of sleep, whereas going to sleep between midday and 5 p.m. leads to shiftworkers' having only about a quarter of normal sleep (Folkard, 1996). Going to sleep after 8 a.m. leads to five hours' or less sleep. The reasons for the sleep loss are probably due to a variety of factors: body rhythms, more noise in the day, and the desire to be sociable when other people are around, amongst others. It has also been suggested that sleeping at non-usual times is more fragmented, shallower and less restful (Campbell, 1992). The loss of sleep builds up over the time a person is working the shift rota, leading to a cumulative sleep debt.

Latent performance deficits

The preceding sections have outlined, in the main, the direct effects of workload, environmental stressors, states of the individual, and time of day on performance. One of the most surprising aspects of research findings into mental performance is that although there are direct effects they are often difficult to demonstrate. Hockey (1996) observes that 'in relation to workload, manifest breakdown in primary task skill under externally imposed stress is unusual, and rarely greater than 10 percent of normal functional levels'.

There is a common subjective observation that as a task gets more demanding it is possible to put more effort into it to maintain performance. This subjective feeling has received empirical support. Wilkinson (1962) found that when asked to do an adding task, sleep-deprived people increased their muscle tension. The interesting thing, though, was that those whose muscle tension increased most were the ones whose performance was least impaired. Those whose muscle tension increased least were the ones whose performance, in terms of both speed and accuracy, was most affected. The notion used to explain this and similar findings is that people use **compensatory effort** to maintain task performance. The consequence of using compensatory effort is that there are fewer mental resources available, and this can leave the person more vulnerable to disruption if additional demands are made. The latter can be termed latent degradation.

Hockey (1996) details four possible patterns of latent degradation, which in effect summarise many observations made of psychophysiological changes under conditions of workload, environmental and state influences. The four patterns are secondary decrement, strategic adjustment, compensatory costs and aftereffects.

Secondary decrements were discussed in relation to mental workload. Essentially they are reduced efficiencies on secondary aspects of performance, or on imposed secondary tasks. In addition to being found as a consequence of workload they are also found as a result of environmental conditions such as noise, and as a result of fatigue and sleep loss.

Strategic adjustment reflects the use of simpler or less effortful mental processing in the face of high demands, preserving primary task goals at the expense of other demands. Hockey cites the increasing selectivity of attention as one example, and the shift, when in noise, to faster but less accurate responding as another. Sperandio (1978) found changes in the way air traffic controllers handled their work when the number of aircraft they had to deal with rose beyond the controller's typical limit. Under high load the controllers adopted a routinised procedure for all aircraft, instead of individualised routeing of each aircraft. Hockey suggests that this change reflects a move to reduce dependency on the limited working memory resource.

Compensatory costs are related to the compensatory effort discussed above. Two general kinds of interrelated effects can be distinguished: increased activation in energetic psychophysiological processes, and increases in subjective effort and strain. An example of how these effects occur comes from a study by Lundberg and Frankenhaeuser (1978). They found noise impaired performance in one study but not another, and the findings were associated with different patterns of cost. When performance was maintained, levels of adrenaline and subjective effort increased, in contrast to when noise impaired performance. Interestingly, Rissler and Jacobson (1987) found that the implementation of a new computer system in an organisation led to a period of over-time and time pressure. Performance was not impaired but adrenaline and cognitive effort were increased.

Hockey makes the point that compensatory effort and its regulation is, at least partly, under the control of the individual rather than the task or environment. As was discussed previously, fatigue can be thought of as a feeling of an 'aversion to further effort'. An option in these circumstances is to disengage from primary task goals.

After-effects have either not been looked for much, or, in the case of fatigue, not found consistently (Broadbent, 1979). Clearly, when the primary task is finished, a fatigue test, or a new set of circumstances, can appear novel and interesting, and because of that, mask any costs associated with maintaining the primary task. Holding (1983) showed that after many hours' work, when given a choice, people may elect to pursue risky but low-effort strategies. However, more research is needed into after-effects to establish the nature of the cost carry-over from effortful maintenance of primary task performance.

Task allocation

One of the important technological system design decisions taken concerns **task allocation**: what functions the technology will perform and what functions the operator will carry out. The tendency in many complex technological systems, especially those using computer control, is to implement what is called '**supervisory control**'. Control is automated to a very high degree. The technology does most of the active operation of machinery, and the operator is placed in a monitoring role, with additional responsibility for when things go wrong. Examples of this kind of control abound in aviation, chemical and nuclear processing, and computerised manufacturing processes. In aviation, much of the flying is done on 'automatic pilot'. With advanced manufacturing technology, operators load raw materials into machines, which are then processed by robot handling and machines controlled by computer (Chmiel and Wall, 1994). The consequences of this kind of automation are at least twofold. First, the design 'fixes' the allocation of tasks and roles between the operator and technology in advance; allocating functions in this way takes no account of variations in workload, changes in the environment, and the changes in the state of the individual, all of which are liable to occur. Second, removing the operator from active control of the system has the unwanted side-effect of reducing his or her understanding of how the system works in terms of cause and effect. An impoverished awareness of cause and effect relationships potentially raises serious problems in emergency situations.

Effective function allocation depends, in part, on a thorough analysis of the tasks the technology and person have to do. Obviously the methods detailed in Chapter 2 are important. However, Hancock and Scallen (1996) suggest that it is not easy to specify what a task is, precisely because tasks are dependent on the person performing them, and the context within which they occur. Context here means the goals for the system as well as the environment. Hancock and Scallen therefore argue that allocation is directly dependent on the level of detail to which the goals, strategies, tasks and actions are specified. They suggest that 'the everyday designer has found the sterile, machine-oriented descriptions of human and machine abilities so static and underspecified, that any attempt to enact function allocation in practice has proved a frustrating and unrewarding exercise'. They go on to say that specifying and fixing allocation in advance (static allocation) 'often require detailed and predictive inputs concerning the environment as well as specification of all possible constraints. Neither of these requirements is at all realistic, even for only moderately complex systems.'

Hancock and Scallen (1996) propose that static allocation is seriously flawed because it fosters a division between person and technology, is inflexible, devalues a flexible response to unusual situations, and diminishes operator understanding. They argue that function allocation should move away from static to dynamic task allocation, where allocation decisions can be made during the execution of system tasks. For example, the technology could detect when the operator was becoming overloaded, or bored, and switch allocation accordingly. The notion then becomes one of technology and the operator's sharing and exchanging tasks, resulting in the operator's being more active in the control of the system.

Summary

This chapter has considered the relationship between technology and people from the point of view of the person as a processor of information, and the technology as imposing mental, rather than physical, demands on the person. Mental workload was discussed, and theories about mental capacity were outlined in terms of processing resources and informational limits. Theoretically and practically based methods for measuring work-load were presented. Thereafter variability in mental processing efficiency was considered, especially in terms of aspects of the environment, changes in the state of the individual, and as a function of time of day and circadian rhythms. Traditional and developing approaches to function allocation in technological system design were then reviewed.

Chapter 5

Work safety in complex technological systems

■ Accidents at work   93

■ Individuals and safety behaviour   94

■ Human error   95

■ Accidents, error and stress   98

■ Violations of safety procedures   100
Risk perception   100
Attitudes to safety   102

■ Personality   103

■ Technological systems, organisations
and safety   104
Disasters   104

■ Organisational safety practices   107
Safety programmes   107
Safety climate   108

■ Error management in technological
systems   109
Human reliability studies   109
Error-tolerant systems   110
Error reduction   111

■ Summary   112

THIS CHAPTER CONSIDERS safety when working with technology, and in particular concentrates on the psychological influences apparent in accidents and system breakdowns. Errors and failures cost money, even if they do not result in personal injury to the worker, but at the extreme, errors can cause considerable damage to people and the environment. The chapter first of all explores individual human error, and then discusses how work and organisational factors contribute to technological systems failures and safety.

The complexity and efficiency of modern technology in many industries depend upon computerisation and automation. Control rooms in nuclear power stations and chemical processing plants in the UK are almost invariably based on computer control and display of the plant processes. In manufacturing, advanced technology utilising robots and computer control has begun to dominate. Even in jobs where traditional human skills are needed, such as intensive care and antenatal medicine, electronic equipment and displays are used.

The demand placed on human operators by this technology is largely mental rather than physical, and this gives rise to important questions: What do operators understand of the system and technology they control? How does automation affect this understanding, and the cognitive nature of the control task? How much capacity do operators have in dealing with mental workload? What happens when fatigue sets in? Is understanding of routine operations sufficient in an emergency situation? How does stress affect cognitive processing? All these questions are the subject of ongoing research, driven by the need to make hazardous complex systems safe, and technological systems efficient.

So far, research has shown that people are limited such that their mental capacities can be overloaded. Automating part of the technology can help with this, but introduces its own problems because the task changes from being active to being predominantly passive, where operators monitor equipment rather than control it. The change means factors like sustained attention and boredom become important, with consequent lapses of attention likely to produce error. Understanding routine operations may utilise different skills and cognitive processes in contrast to coping with emergency situations, and stress can further alter how the work task is mentally processed (Wickens, 1992).

Accidents at work

Industrial sectors differ in the types and severity of accidents incurred in them. The UK Health and Safety Executive (HSE) reported that for the period 1987 to 1990, railway staff suffered four times as many accidental deaths, as a proportion of those at risk, as the chemical and allied industries. In clothing and footware manufacture death rates were more than 60 times less than in the manufacture of bricks, pottery, glass, cement, etc. One of the highest rates was in the offshore oil and gas sector.

How can the causes of fatalities and other injuries at work be understood?

Brown (1990) proposes that reporting accidents is the only practical way of evaluating system safety under real operating conditions, and of identifying factors which may be contributing to accident causation. He defines an accident as the 'unplanned outcome of inappropriate behaviour'. The important distinction made by this definition is that between **antecedent behaviour** and the consequences of the behaviour. In other words, workers can be engaged in unsafe actions which may or may not lead to injury, or technological breakdowns.

Brown (1990) argues that, to be useful, accident reporting systems at work should highlight primary safety improvements; capture antecedent behaviour; avoid subjectivity; avoid apportioning blame; detail task and system demands; collect data on all accidents regardless of their consequences; and detail the nature, severity and causes of accidental injury. Many accident reporting systems do not approach these ideals. Often accident reporting is based on retrospective verbal accounts in reaction to an injury or death, rather than near-misses and other accidents. Accounts of behaviour leading up to an accident are frequently given after the event, and thus rely on memory. (The 'black box' flight recorders fitted to aircraft are notable exceptions.) As an outcome, accident investigations often find someone to blame, rather than concentrate on the complexity of the causes.

The consequences of accidents at work include injury to workers, lost production, disruption to working patterns, the ruination of machinery, and economic and legislative outcomes such as compensation claims. In recent times industrial injury has been at the centre of national policies concerning these issues, and there are various laws governing them. In the UK the HSE plays a considerable role in monitoring and enforcing safety standards at work, and in the USA a similar function is carried out by the Occupational Safety and Health Administration (OSHA).

The UK Health and Safety Commission produced regulations in 1992 governing the 'Management of Health and Safety at Work'. The regulations state that every employer should make a sufficient assessment of the risks to health and safety to employees he or she is responsible towards. Risk includes the likelihood that harm will occur, and its severity.

A psychological perspective on safety at work gives rise to two main questions: What is the relationship between individual perceptions, attitudes and cognition to safety behaviour and technological system failures? and, What are the effects of organisational procedures, culture and standards on safety?

Individuals and safety behaviour

The relationship of individual characteristics to safe behaviour has been investigated from two quite distinct perspectives: on the one hand social psychology, and on the other **cognitive psychology**. The cognitive psychology tradition focuses on human error performance as a function of mental processing operations, and the social psychology tradition concentrates on personality, attitudes and perceptions. Both traditions have thrown up interesting information on safety at work.

Human error

Human error, as a field of enquiry, is concerned with why people make mistakes, or forget to do critical parts of their job. The approach concentrates more on the function of cognitive processes in relation to error. It is a growing field of activity. Part of the reason for the interest in human error is that it derives from a tradition that views people as processors of information, and the understanding of how people interact with technology, particularly with computers, has been well served by this approach. Many safety-critical systems can be viewed as providing the people in them with considerable amounts of information which they need to perceive, remember, decide about and take action on. Thus human error has frequently been informed by studies in the nuclear, chemical and aviation industries. However, the principles that have been discovered from such studies apply to many work settings where technology is employed to present information and control activities.

An essential starting-point in investigating error is to understand what errors themselves are. Obviously it would be very difficult to examine each and every error a person made, as if each mistake were somehow unique; a sensible starting-point is to ask whether errors fall into a few categories, where each category has distinctive characteristics. That is, we should try to devise a taxonomy of errors. Many proposals for a taxonomy have been put forward which relate the errors observed to underlying mental processes. Freud, for example, proposed that slips of the tongue were a product of the subconscious. Bartlett (1932) suggested that errors in recalling stories were due to relating new material to old knowledge, structured in schemata. Recall tended to make the stories more regular, meaningful and conventionalised than they had been originally.

More modern theorists have put forward a taxonomy which has gained wide acceptance among those considering the impact of technology on safety. Reason (1990) proposes a taxonomy which divides unsafe acts into two broad categories: activities that are unintentional, and those that are intended. Unintended actions are further broken down into slips and lapses, and intended actions into mistakes and violations. Much of Reason's analysis is based on diary studies of everyday errors, and case studies of large-scale technological disasters such as that at the Chernobyl nuclear power station in the then USSR. Reason's taxonomy accords closely with that put forward at approximately the same time by Norman (1988), which drew on observations of everyday actions.

An attraction of Reason's conceptualisation is that errors are explicitly related to cognitive functioning. Slips and lapses are defined as errors which result from some failure in the execution and/or storage of an action sequence, regardless of whether the plan which guided them was adequate to achieve its objective.

Mistakes, on the other hand, are defined as deficiencies or failures in the judgemental and/or inferential processes involved in the selection of an objective, or in how to achieve it, irrespective of whether the actions necessary to realise the objective run according to plan.

Violations, in contrast, are seen not as breakdowns in normal cognitive processing, but as deliberate flouting of safety procedures and rules.

Reason (1990) terms slips, lapses and mistakes basic error types. There are numerous documented examples of error types from incidents in the nuclear power industry. At the Davis-Besse (1985) plant in the USA, an operator, wanting to start the steam and feedwater rupture control system manually, inadvertently pressed the wrong two buttons on the control panel (a slip). At Chernobyl a previous operator error had reduced reactor power to well below 10 per cent of maximum. Despite strict safety procedures which prohibited any operation below 20 per cent of maximum power, a team of electrical engineers and operators continued with a planned test programme, contributing to a double explosion within the reactor core (a mistake).

Reason further refined his conceptualisation of error types by relating them to a hierarchy of performance levels developed by Rasmussen over several years (e.g. 1986). Rasmussen studied, initially, workers engaged in fault-finding in electronic components using a verbal protocol technique. **Verbal protocols** are obtained by asking the person to explain what they are, or were, doing. Rasmussen's insight was to analyse activity relevant to industrial settings in terms of skill-, rule- or knowledge-based performance levels. The levels reflect decreasing familiarity with the activity and situation. The skill-based level is concerned with routine actions in a familiar operating environment. At the other extreme, knowledge-based performance is required in novel situations and circumstances, and is dependent on problem-solving to work out and decide on a course of action. Rule-based performance is where a situation or set of circumstances has been encountered before, and where the action needed is governed by rules of the form IF (situation) THEN (action).

Slips and lapses are thus errors at the skill-based level. Mistakes are refined into two types: rule-based and knowledge-based.

Reason (1990) views error types as arising out of fundamentally useful mental processes, rather than maladaptive tendencies. Further, his analysis suggests that the basic error types manifest themselves as a result of mental information processing by which 'stored knowledge structures are selected and retrieved in response to current situational demands'. In short, basic errors are tied in to the context present at the time, and result from attentional, memory and inferential failures.

Skill-based errors are associated with inattention or overattention (consciously interrupting automatic activities). Rule-based errors are associated with the misapplication of good rules, or the application of bad rules. Knowledge-based errors are associated with the limitations of human ability to solve problems and reason with new circumstances, for example the poor ability to reason rationally, or to hold very many bits of information in mind at the same time.

Reason's analysis proposes that mistakes are much harder to detect than slips and lapses, because, he argues, consciousness is tuned to departures from intentions. Mistakes, because they are intended actions, for whatever reason, can go unnoticed for long periods. Such a view is supported by studies on nuclear power operator teams grappling with simulated plant failures (Woods, 1984). In all, nearly two-thirds of errors went undetected. Half of the execution errors (slips and lapses) were detected by the crews themselves, whereas none of the state identification failures (rule- and knowledge-based mistakes) was.

Reason (1990) does not have much to say about violations. His main concern lies with errors that arise from cognitive processing, rather than deliberate non-compliance with safety procedures. However, violations in themselves have interesting psychological aspects which have been studied from a more social psychological perspective, and will be discussed later in the chapter.

The relationship between errors and accidents at work is by no means clear. The discussion earlier in the chapter should make it apparent that antecedent behaviour and its consequences are two distinguishable factors. It is possible to commit an error, but for that error not to lead to an accident. In a study on the time of day, errors and fatal accidents at work, Williamson and Feyer (1995) show that accidents demonstrate much more variation across 24 hours than do knowledge-, rule- and skill-based errors. In short, there was no direct correspondence between the time when most accidents occurred and errors.

Accidents, error and stress

Conceptually it is sensible to suggest that workplace stress will have an impact on accidents and error. Of course, in order to examine the effect of stress itself, it is necessary to hold a number of other aspects of jobs and tasks constant. However, this is very hard to do. Some jobs are inherently more dangerous than others (deep-sea diving compared to office typing, for example), and this could produce more accidents and feelings of stress. There is a large amount of research now on what aspects of workplaces produce feelings of stress, but there are not many studies which relate feeling stressed to accidents.

A different tack is to treat conditions at work as stressors and examine their effects on performance, accidents and errors. The workplace can involve various environmental and social conditions, such as noise and heat, long hours and fatigue, and pressure to complete work to time deadlines. It is important to investigate whether these types of factors are involved in accidents and human error.

Again, it is extremely difficult to research answers to the question of how stressors affect error at work. First, because factors such as fatigue are difficult to manipulate, and second, because the question demands studying moment-by-moment fluctuations in, say, time pressure, and its effect on error, and this is very hard to do in the workplace. Laboratory studies of environmental stressors on performance were discussed in Chapter 4.

An approach adopted by Reason and Mycielska (1982) offers some insight, however. They asked 63 university students to keep a diary to record their slips and lapses over a continuous period of 7 days. As soon as possible after recording a slip or lapse, the students were asked to complete a set of standard ratings, including how well they felt, whether they felt tired, and whether they were in familiar surroundings. Reason (1988) summarised the results from this and other diary studies as showing a relatively consistent picture associated with everyday **cognitive failures**. When slips occurred respondents were 'carrying out some highly automatized task in very familiar surroundings', and they were distracted by something in their immediate vicinity, or preoccupied by some inner concern. However, they were not feeling particularly upset, emotional or unwell, and neither did they feel that environmental factors such as noise, temperature or poor illumination contributed to cognitive failure. On the other hand, fatigue and time pressure were rated as influential on some occasions, but not on others.

Violations of safety procedures

Violations are the intentional breaking of safety procedures and rules by workers. Sabotage is the most extreme reason for violating established rules, but procedures are ignored for many reasons not to do with any desire to wreak havoc and mayhem. This section will not consider sabotage, but will discuss the views about why workers do not comply with safety procedures and engage in unsafe behaviour.

Risk perception

A possible influence on why workers do not comply with safety procedures could be that they do not perceive any risk associated with the situation they are in, and/or with other courses of action. In the health field investigation of subjective beliefs concerning hazards suggests that the likelihood of a person engaging in preventive behaviour is a function of their perception of risk involved in an activity, their belief about whether the outcome is serious or not, and whether they believe they can do something to prevent the outcome (Rosenstock, 1974). Self-protective behaviour depends in part on a person's subjective estimate of risk.

Risk can be defined in many ways. Two possibilities are 'probability of undesired consequences' and 'weight of undesired consequences (loss) relative to comparable possible desired consequences (gain)'. In a report to the Royal Society, reviewing the research on risk perception since 1983, Pidgeon et al. (1992) suggest that risk is appropriately defined as 'threat to people and things they value'.

Pidgeon et al. (1992) argue that it is difficult to separate objective and subjective risk since all risk assessments involve human judgement and social, cultural and political influences, and that risk perception is a multidimensional concept because particular hazards mean different things to different social groups. Investigation in the oil and gas industry has shown that different groups of workers perceived the same hazards differently in terms of risk and safety (Mearns and Flin, 1996).

Risk perception involves attention to, and processing of, a diverse range of information relating to hazards. The information can be gained through direct experience of hazards or through sources like the mass media, scientific communications or fellow workers. Goldberg *et al.* (1991) proposed that information about potential threats was assimilated by workers through formal and informal learning both inside and outside the workplace, and through direct and indirect experience of accidents. They found that key factors relating to perception of threat were training, and experience specific to the task being performed.

Psychometric studies of attitudes to hazards have shown that people distinguish between risks to individuals and risks to society. Green (1979), cited in Pidgeon *et al.* (1992), found that risk perceptions could be measured by two scales: personal safety and threat to society. Slovic *et al.* (1980) asked people to rate 90 hazards (for example nuclear power, chemical fertilisers, caffeine) with respect to 18 characteristics. Their responses reflected three factors: dread risk (i.e. how uncontrollable and catastrophic the risk was); unknown risk (i.e. how unobservable the risk was); and number of people exposed (including degree of personal exposure). Slovic *et al.* concluded that perceptions of risk were related to where the risk was in relation to these three factors, and that the most important factor was 'dread risk': the higher a hazard scored on this factor the more people wanted to see the risk reduced, and controlled through regulation. The hazard scoring highest was nuclear weapons. Subsequent research has shown that the qualitative dimensions that are important for risk perception differ for different hazards. So, for example, Gardner and Gould (1989) found that 'catastrophic potential' was important for nuclear and chemical technologies, but less so for air and car travel.

Researchers have also considered risk perception from the perspective of mental judgements about the probability of events, ignoring for the most part emotional and motivational aspects. The findings from human judgements about uncertain events suggest that people are not rational in their judgements; rather they use cognitive heuristics or 'rules of thumb' to decide whether something is likely to happen or not (Kahneman *et al.*, 1982). The heuristics are a type of cognitive bias, useful for the most part, but likely to lead to systematic error in some circumstances. Experts are not immune to biases either; for example, they have been shown to be overconfident in their judgements (Svenson, 1989).

Attitudes to safety

Individual attitudes to safety, and the degree to which they affect safe behaviour in the workplace, have received relatively little attention. Cox and Cox (1991) studied one European company and suggested that employee attitudes to safety could be structured along five factors which included personal scepticism, individual responsibility and personal immunity. Personal scepticism involved cynical perceptions towards the importance of safety, individual responsibility referred to the responsibility that people feel they have for working safely, and personal immunity involved the belief that accidents could be avoided as a result of personal expertise and experience.

Attitudes such as these can be fitted readily into a framework of the categories involved in the causes of accidents proposed by Dejoy (1986) in relation to planning health education strategies. Dejoy outlines three categories: predisposing, enabling and reinforcing. Predisposing factors are personal characteristics such as beliefs, attitudes, values and perceptions that affect self-protective behaviour, for example personal scepticism. Enabling factors are characteristics of the work environment or system that promote or block safe behaviour, for example training and knowledge. Reinforcing factors refer to actual or expected rewards or punishment as a consequence of the behaviour, for example management support. Questionnaire studies have shown the usefulness of the framework in understanding the factors involved in employees' intentions to comply with safety procedures in work organisations in both the UK and Asia (Smallwood, 1994; Charuwatee, 1996).

Personality

In this context personality typically refers to a relatively enduring, stable disposition. Early in the twentieth century a study of accidents in munitions factories in England during the First World War found that the majority of accidents involved relatively few people. This observation gave rise to the idea of 'accident proneness', that certain people have a disposition to accidents, a concept which has captured the popular imagination. However, subsequent research has tended not to support the idea that there is a stable personality trait of being accident-prone; rather, different people go through periods of being more prone (Reason, 1974). Generally the highest accident rates are found in young and inexperienced workers. It has been suggested that the reasons behind this observation are that young people are more impulsive and inattentive, and have less family responsibility than older workers. However, using the term 'proneness' has been criticised because it places too little emphasis on contributory factors outside the person. McKenna (1983) suggests that the term 'differential accident liability' should be used instead.

In terms of differential liability, several questionnaire-based studies have shown that over periods of several months some people are rated, or rate themselves, as more liable to minor 'cognitive failures' (Reason, 1988). Cognitive failures are failing to carry out intended actions (i.e. slips and lapses); for example, entering the living room to get a book, and instead finding yourself turning the television on. These kinds of failures tend to be associated with being distracted or preoccupied with something at the time.

Another aspect of personality which has been studied in the safety context is locus of control. Locus of control (Rotter, 1966) ranges from internal to external. Those who are internal expect their actions to affect what happens to them and others. Externals believe they have little influence on events. Jones and Wuebker (1985) developed a safety locus of control scale and demonstrated that people in lower-risk groups were more internally oriented. Wuebker (1986) further reported that externally oriented employees appeared to have more accidents.

Technological systems, organisations and safety

Disasters

Several of the major incidents that could have had potentially catastrophic consequences for the world, like the nuclear near-meltdown at Three Mile Island (TMI) in the USA and the Chernobyl catastrophe in the USSR, have been, at least in part, attributed to human error when operating complex systems. However, in analyses of most of the major disasters in the 1970s and 1980s Reason (1990) has demonstrated that many features of work organisations contribute to the breakdown of complex technological systems. Understanding safe working with technology involves therefore much more than investigating why individuals engage in unsafe acts. The organisational and system structures and procedures must also be considered.

Three Mile Island

At Three Mile Island, 16 km south of Harrisburg, Pennsylvania, the flow of water to Unit No. 2's nuclear reactor secondary heat removal system was interrupted. The feedwater pumps had shut down as a result of maintenance engineers' accidently introducing a small amount of moisture into the plant's instrument air system. The moisture interrupted the air pressure to two valves on the pumps. Emergency feedwater pumps came on automatically, but did not work as planned because water supplying the pumps was blocked by valves left shut in error during maintenance operations a couple of days earlier. This meant that heat was not being removed from the primary coolant round the reactor core, leading to a quick rise in core temperature and pressure. Another automatic safety device then came into operation, stopping the chain reaction. However, the decaying radioactive materials still produced heat, and the temperature and pressure increased further in the core. The pressure was designed to be relieved automatically through a pilot-operated relief valve (PORV), which when open would allow water to pass from the core through a pressuriser vessel into a sump below the reactor. The PORV should have opened, relieved the pressure, and then shut automatically. Unfortunately, only 13 seconds into the emergency the PORV stuck open, which meant that pressurised radioactive water was pouring out of the core.

The time was 4 a.m. on 28 March 1979. The emergency caused alarm lights to flash, and an auditory alarm to sound in the control room. For the following two hours or so the control room operators tried to get to grips with the cause of the alarm. During the course of this activity the operators actually cut back the injection of water into the reactor coolant, reducing the flow rate from approximately 1000 to 25 gallons per minute, thus causing serious core damage. The emergency lasted more than 16 hours in total.

As a consequence of the incident there was a serious risk of a 'meltdown', or that hazardous radiation could escape from the plant. Neither of these things happened, although a small amount of radioactive material did escape into the atmosphere, but the incident cost millions of dollars, and the USA halted all further building of nuclear power plants.

The report of the analysis of the causes of the incident attributed a number of errors to the control room staff, but highlighted inadequate control room design, procedures and training rather than inadequacies on the part of operators.

Accident investigators observed that the control panel presented operators with too much complex data: 1600 displays and gauges had to be scanned when the alarm sounded to try to establish the source of the problem. At the time there were already 200 flashing displays and gauges, making the diagnosis of the fault difficult. In addition, the control panel did not contain certain critical information, especially the fact that the PORV had not closed, allowing coolant to escape and uncover the reactor core. The panel had an indicator relating to the PORV, but this showed only whether the valve had been commanded shut or not. It did not indicate the actual status of the valve. This could have been discovered by looking at a drain tank water level indicator, but this was positioned behind the main controls.

A further problem was that the back-up valves – which, if open, could have allowed water into the secondary heat removal system – were closed. The fact that they were closed was not recognised by the operators because maintenance tags on the control panel partially obscured the lights indicating their status. In addition, the diagnostic system designed to supply information about the plant used a computer printer. During the incident messages were being transmitted to the printer at around ten to fifteen per second, overloading it. Information was thus not available until later, and just over an hour into the incident the printer jammed, and some data was lost for good.

Maintenance crew had introduced moisture into the instrument air system. This same error had occurred on two previous occasions, but the operating company had not taken steps to prevent its happening again.

Operator training consisted mostly of lectures and work in a reactor simulator, and did not provide an adequate basis for coping with real emergencies. Little feedback was given to trainees, and the training programme was not evaluated sufficiently. Training emphasised the dangers of flooding the core, but this took no account of a simultaneous loss of core coolant.

There had been an incident prior to TMI-2 at the Davis-Besse plant in 1977, where the PORV had stuck open. The incident was investigated by the plant's makers, and by the US Nuclear Regulatory Commission, but the analyses were not collated, and the information regarding appropriate operator action was not communicated widely to the industry. The operators had also interrupted the flow of water to the reactor, but the analyses had been categorised in a publication by the Nuclear Regulatory Commission under 'valve malfunction' rather than 'operator error'.

The illustration from Three Mile Island shows that any discussion of safety at work needs to consider not just unsafe acts and accidents by and to individuals, but errors and failures at the design and organisational levels, which potentially could form the antecedents to industrial calamities such as that at Three Mile Island. It is the advent of complex technological systems, particularly in the nuclear, aviation, chemical and manufacturing industries, which gives impetus to the study of human and systems error, because the consequences of such error can be on a large scale indeed, as the incident in 1986 at the Chernobyl nuclear power plant in Ukraine so emphatically illustrates.

Reason (1990) divides the contributions people make to system accidents into two broad categories: latent and active errors. Latent errors are present in a system as a result of decisions taken by management and regulatory bodies; active errors are unsafe acts taken for a variety of psychological reasons. Large-scale disasters in complex systems are often the result of combinations of active and latent errors, and inadequate safeguards against possible errors. Reason suggests that possible factors which contribute to fallible management decision-making about safety arise because production goals are balanced against safety goals. Production goals are easily measured, very visible, and when met are rewarded positively. Safety goals, on the other hand, are measured by the absence of accidents, and are highly visible only following an accident or near-miss.

Organisational safety practices

Safety programmes

The procedures and attitudes of organisations to work safety influence the degree of hazard at work. It is no accident that industries with a very good record on safety are those such as aviation and chemicals, where safety is seen as of paramount importance, and where there are many safety-oriented regulations governing work practices. Safety programmes are designed to increase safety at work, and to overcome reasons for unsafe behaviour in workers.

Safety programmes have tended to concentrate on worker training in safe procedures. Thus employees learn about the procedures and the way to carry them out. However, simply knowing a procedure does not mean that a worker will comply with it, so that instituting organisational means to increase safety is also important. One technique which has been demonstrated to be effective uses behaviour modification principles. Haynes *et al.*

(1982) reduced accident rates in bus drivers working in urban transport by 25 per cent using a safety behaviour modification programme. First, safety performance feedback was made public by posting drivers' safety records in the lunchroom. Second, drivers were put into teams that competed against each other's safety record. This meant that the reward related to the group rather than an individual. Finally, winning drivers and teams were given cash and prizes for outstanding safety records. Thus safe behaviour was rewarded. The reward need not be so obvious. Merely posting safety records and publicly recognising good safety performance has also produced increases in safety.

Safety climate

A close link has been observed between the success of safety programmes and **safety climate** (Zohar, 1980). Other research has shown that groups with a 'safety climate' had safer work areas. Work groups with experienced and organised leaders were related to fewer accidents (Butler and Jones, 1979).

Safety climate is measured by eliciting worker perceptions about organisational commitment to safety, such as the perceived importance of safety training, management's attitudes to safety, and so on.

Zohar (1980) found several organisational characteristics that distinguished production companies with high and low accident rates. A consistent factor in low-accident companies was management commitment to safety, manifested, for example, by the personal involvement of top management in routine safety activities, and by safety being given a high priority in company meetings and production scheduling. A second factor was the importance given to safety training. A third factor was the existence of open communication and frequent contact between workers and management. A fourth characteristic of low-accident companies was 'good housekeeping', namely orderly plant operations and high usage of safety devices. Companies with good safety records also had distinctive ways of promoting safety. These included the use of guidance and counselling rather than admonition and enforcement; praise and recognition for safe job performance; and enlisting workers' families in safety promotions. Through examination of the organisational characteristics Zohar (1980) developed eight dimensions of safety climate:

● the importance of safety training programmes;
● management attitudes towards safety;
● effects of safe conduct on promotion;
● the level of risk in the workplace;
● the pace of work demands related to safety;
● the status of the safety officer;
● the effects of safe conduct on social status;
● the status of the safety committee.

Subsequent investigators have boiled down the measurement of safety climate to just two factors: workers' perceptions of management commitment to safety, and workers' involvement in safety (Dedobbeleer and Beland, 1991).

Error management in technological systems

Naturally enough, many companies are motivated or regulated to produce safe working conditions and systems. In hazardous, safety-critical environments such as nuclear power, chemical processing and aviation a strong emphasis has been placed on safety. Two distinct approaches to making technological work systems safer can be distinguished. The first attempts to assess how reliable workers are at what they do, and design the system accordingly. The second approach accepts that people vary in their performance, and that inevitably they will make errors. Therefore the system itself should take the human factor into account, and be designed with human fallibility in mind.

Human reliability studies

The flavour of the first approach can be gained by considering one of the techniques involved. THERP stands for 'technique for human error rate prediction' (Swain and Weston, 1988). The approach taken is to treat the person in the same way as equipment, a valve for example, and to assess how likely it is that the person will fail given a particular operating condition. The human error probability (HEP) is expressed as a ratio of the number of errors made on a task to the number of opportunities for errors. Preferably the HEP assessment is based on actual performance. However, performance data is often lacking, and the assessment is made through an analyst's judgement, or from simulator studies. Once HEPs are obtained for various tasks or procedures they can be combined systematically. The objective of THERP is to relate the probability of human error to system failures, either including or excluding other factors such as equipment functioning that influence system behaviour. Although the human reliability approach is attractive, the various techniques have several shortcomings (Wickens, 1992). First, they ignore human cognitive functioning. Second, assessments rely heavily on expert opinion rather than performance data. Third, treating people in the same way as equipment ignores the fact that people often correct their own errors, whereas when machines fail they are repaired or replaced by others. Fourth, when people make an error, that in itself may affect the likelihood of a subsequent error. The view summarised by Reason (1990) is that human reliability analysis has some way to go before it can be considered a reliable and valid approach.

Error-tolerant systems

Perrow (1984, 1994) argues that system accidents are 'normal' in the sense that however hard the attempts to avoid them are, serious accidents are inevitable. However, Perrow identifies particular types of system where 'normal' accidents will happen. The systems are complex, and tightly coupled. Complexity refers to a system having many different parts, and where the parts interconnect with each other in non-straightforward ways. In contrast, systems could be linear, like an assembly line, and/or simple. Tight coupling implies that the system has only one method of achieving its goals, has invariant sequences, has little slack in it in terms of supplies, equipment or personnel, and that delays in processing are not possible. Systems which fall into this category are aircraft, nuclear plants and chemical plants, according to Perrow.

It follows from Perrow's analysis that making a system error-tolerant means either making it less complex, and/or making it less tightly coupled.

Error reduction

A key reason for studying error is to try to reduce it. Considerable effort has gone into equipment design, system design and safety procedures. From the psychological perspective reviewed in this chapter several ways to reduce error suggest themselves. The key premise behind the suggestions is that errors arise because of a mismatch between the properties of a system as a whole, and the characteristics of human information processing.

Norman (1988) proposes, *inter alia*, that a good conceptual model of the system be promoted on the part of its users, and that the structure of tasks be simplified to minimise the load on vulnerable cognitive processes such as planning and problem-solving. He also suggests that constraints on what system users can do should be designed in with safety in mind, and that the system should be designed to make error recovery possible.

Frese (1987) suggests that training should allow people to make mistakes so that they can learn from them. Training should encourage and support an active, exploratory approach to the system. Training in a simulator could try to create emergency scenarios as well as normal operations to give operators experience they could draw on in a real emergency. Unfortunately it is very difficult to foresee, and hence simulate, what real emergencies might entail.

Others have suggested that external aids, like memory prompts, be part of the system support.

Summary

This chapter has sought to outline the main psychological approaches to safety in work settings, with an emphasis on technological work systems. Accidents were distinguished in terms of antecedent behaviours and consequences. Psychological approaches to safety at work have been informed by cognitive and social psychology. Human error was discussed in terms of its relationship to cognitive processing of information. Errors were divided into those that were the result of unintended and intended actions respectively. Unintended actions were slips and lapses, and were related to attention and memory failures. Intended actions were rule- or knowledge-based mistakes, and were related to inferential processes. Violations of safety procedures were discussed in relation to perceptions and attitudes towards hazards and safety from a social psychology perspective. Organisational and systems approaches to safety discussed how organisational culture influences safety behaviour, and how error analyses could explain technological systems disasters. Finally, various influences on how work organisations and systems could be made safer were outlined.

Chapter 6

Team-working
and technology

■ Socio-technical systems 115

■ Computer-supported co-operative
work 117

■ Distributed cognition 119

■ Social aspects of working in groups 122
Group development 123
Groups and decision-making 123
Team-working and performance 124
Leadership and group-working 125
Work groups 127

■ Summary 132

TEAM-WORKING IS ATTRACTING enormous interest among managers and human resource departments of many different kinds of organisations. Part of the interest is the view that groups hold the potential for increasing both productivity and employee satisfaction.

Technology and group-working are relatively recent bedfellows. The philosophy of 'scientific management', described in Chapter 2, meant that technology could be seen as a means of automating simplified jobs in order to gain economic benefit (Braverman, 1974). However, the expected benefit from technology was not often realised. For example, in 1952 automatic looms were introduced into the textile mills belonging to the Ahmedabad Manufacturing and Calico Printing Company in India, in the belief that automation would increase productivity. However, the result was lower productivity and a higher percentage of damaged goods. The technology had been introduced without any change to the old organisational management structure based on scientific management. When workers were asked to suggest changes to the way in which their work was organised, the result was the setting up of autonomous work groups, individuals taking on more varied job tasks, and a flattened management hierarchy. Clearly, the effectiveness of technology depends in part on suitable ways of organising workers to use it.

That social relations, and not just economic self-interest, were important for productivity was demonstrated in one of the most famous series of studies in occupational psychology. We have seen in Chapter 1 that productivity can be stimulated by the presence of researchers at a workplace, as a result of the interest they show in the workers. The same studies, carried out at the Hawthorne plant in Chicago, revealed another interesting finding. This second set of observations involved a group of men. It was noted that the men developed their own informal pattern of social relations and 'norms' for working behaviour. Despite a financial incentive scheme which offered more money for more productivity, the group chose a level of output well below what they were capable of producing.

Although there are many ways in which people form groups at work, for example the works football team or social club, this chapter is concerned with groups or teams that the organisation has instituted formally. Formal groups have an identity and set of functions which relate to the objectives of the organisation. Such groups include quality circles, project teams and autonomous work groups.

There are a number of characteristics essential to defining a work group or team. These include: having shared objectives; having well-defined roles; working together to achieve objectives; having an organisational identity; and having a limited membership, in practice less than about 20 people (West, 1996).

The emphasis in this chapter is on the linking of technology and team-working. However, it should be said at the outset that there is no coherent view about the ways in which group-working and modern computer-based methods of working should be understood. Indeed, it is not yet clear what are the most important questions to ask about the design of technology to complement team-working, and the kinds of ways in which teams should be constituted to utilise technology. The chapter therefore outlines recent and more traditional approaches to the issues involved in teams, and the design and use of technology. The main theme is that groups and technology form a system. The chapter starts therefore with one of the older and well-known approaches, socio-technical systems theory.

Socio-technical systems

Socio-technical systems theory suggested that people and technology be viewed as a system, and that both social and technical parts of the system should be designed optimally. The approach, developed in the 1950s and 1960s, originated at the Tavistock Institute in London.

Trist and Bamforth (1951) compared the impact of a new mechanised method for mining coal with the method that it replaced. The old system had several features including group-working, multiskilling and a sense of autonomy. The new system meant that the old social structure became inoperable, leading to a number of problems at the individual and organisational level, including performance.

One of the central social design principles to emerge was that teams be created around sets of tasks that formed an iden-tifiable whole, for example building a car. These teams were labelled autonomous work groups, and a key characteristic was that the team should be self-managing, whilst working within agreed constraints such as production targets and safety limits. Other design principles proposed, *inter alia*, that methods of working should be minimally specified, but that essential aspects of tasks and the methods needed to carry them out should be identified; and that variances, if they cannot be eliminated, must be controlled as near to their point of origin as possible. Variances are any unprogrammed, or unpredictable, event, such as devia-tions in the quality of raw materials for manufacturing processes, the failure to take action at a critical time, or a machine, or computer, failure. Organisational boundaries should not impede the sharing of information, learning and knowledge; and roles should be multifunctional and multiskilled (Cherns, 1976).

In terms of job design this approach has much in common with the job characteristics model described by Hackman and Oldham (1976) and outlined in more detail in Chapter 2. Hackman (1983) suggested that the two approaches could be integrated, and group work be implemented in the form of 'autonomous work groups' or 'self-managing work teams'.

However, whilst several of the central tenets of socio-tech-nical systems theory have gained acceptance, in practice their implementation has tended to focus on group-working, taking the technology as a given. Thus the design principles themselves concentrate on the social aspects of work organisation, and provide little guide to the design of the technical aspects. Autonomous work groups tend to be implemented around existing technology, and adapted to it, rather than the social and technical parts of the system being jointly optimised.

Computer-supported co-operative work

A different approach to work teams is to consider how the technology can serve the purposes of the work group. Recent interest has focused on how computer technology can be made to serve this purpose. The approach is relatively recent, beginning in the mid-1980s. Computerised information systems promise, in principle, tremendous flexibility in regard to their implementation and use. The question is what is the best way of designing and utilising such technology. Approaches of this kind can be subsumed under the heading of computer-supported co-operative work.

Computer-supported co-operative work (CSCW) is in its infancy at the moment. Olson *et al.* (1993) reviewed the field and outlined a number of pressing gaps in knowledge about how groups and technology interact. First, they state that there is a need for theories and models of the users of technology. Second, they underline the need to understand the nature of group work, in particular how the cognitive and communication abilities of individuals 'blend and progress' in groups. Third, they emphasise the importance of understanding how common knowledge and culture in the organisation, and in particular how a group's organisational history and the roles group members adopt, guide activities.

Johansen (1988) characterised group activities using technology in terms of the dimensions of time and place. Face-to-face meetings occur at the same time and in the same place. Shiftwork happens in the same place but at different times for different groups. Video-conferencing allows a group to talk together at the same time, even though its members are located in different places. Electronic mail facilitates the exchange of information at various times and in different places. Clearly, different technologies meet different activities more or less successfully. Designing and implementing the technology for group activities will require an understanding of what the group goals and tasks are, and how the group is made up.

Chapter 4 discussed some of the individual cognitive and perceptual–motor skills and limitations that people possess, and that are brought to bear when humans interact with machines and computers. Olson *et al.* (1993) also propose that where groups and technology are involved, the technology may need to represent the intentions and actions of others who are not visible to all group members. The design of the technology, therefore, has to take into account more than an individual using it. Issues which require further research, according to Olson *et al.*, include the interface between 'the object of work' and co-workers, and the physical setting, both virtual and real, in which work takes place.

The way in which groups and technology work can be considered from two broad perspectives. The first takes the group as the unit for analysis. Thus group goals, ways of operating, the group's ability to learn and its capabilities are key aspects for study. Important to this view are the ways in which group members co-ordinate their activities, through expectations, norms, learned procedures and communication. Situated action (Suchman, 1987) and distributed cognition (Hutchins, 1995), discussed later in the chapter, are frameworks for theories about how all these elements work together.

The second perspective considers groups as collections of individuals and tries to explain group functioning and effectiveness by considering how individuals contribute to the group in terms of their experiences, how work is divided between group members, how individuals make the transition between their own work and that of the group, and how they communicate their ideas, demands and information to others in the group. Frameworks for understanding groups from this perspective tend to be drawn from the cognitive and social psychology of individuals. The cognitive approach is discussed in detail in Chapter 4.

Distributed cognition

New technology, both computerisation of manufacturing and information technology, has placed considerable emphasis on mental aspects of working. **Distributed cognition**, as an approach, tries to provide an account of how information and the technology that supports it are handled across groups of people. The approach itself is relatively new, and so is at an early stage of development.

Distributed cognition arises from the recognition that previous frameworks are limited in what they offer for understanding the workings of collaborative cognitive activity, such as problem-solving and decision-making, *in situ*. For example, traditional cognitive psychology has tended to examine individual, discrete cognitions and actions in the laboratory, thus missing out the dynamic, collaborative and contextual aspects of new technology at work. On the other hand, social and organisational approaches have used ethnographic methods to examine, for example, teams working with new technology in control centres used in air traffic control, and at airports (e.g. Suchman, 1993). However, there are doubts that the design of new technology could benefit from a purely sociological analysis, because cognitive aspects are sidelined.

Distributed cognition aims to explain cognitive activities in settings that are culturally constituted (Hutchins, 1995), such as work and workplaces. The perspective taken is summarised by the assertion Hutchins makes that

> In terms of the energy budget of a human group and the efficiency with which a group exploits its physical environment, social organisational factors often produce group properties that differ considerably from the properties of individuals. Clearly, the same sorts of phenomena occur in the cognitive domain. Depending on their organisation, groups must have cognitive properties that are not predictable from a knowledge of the properties of the individuals in a group. The emphasis on finding and describing 'knowledge structures' that are somewhere 'inside'

an individual encourages us to overlook the fact that human cognition is always situated in a complex sociocultural world and cannot be unaffected by it. (1995, p. xiii)

Distributed cognition emphasises knowledge and information resources as key aspects of group work with technology. Viewed from the point of view of a functional system which includes team members and the technology, the focus is on the way in which knowledge is transmitted between team members, and how information is processed through the technology. An underlying assumption made about the functional system is that it will have cognitive properties that are different from those of individuals. Individuals themselves will differ in the amount and kind of knowledge they share, and in the knowledge unique to them.

An important issue is how knowledge and information are transformed by work activities. For example, information displayed on a computer screen will be changed by an operator keying in a command to the computer. Another example is where an operator's understanding concerning an activity is changed by a work colleague telling him or her a new piece of information.

In distributed cognition it becomes important to understand how knowledge is transmitted through the system, and how it supports the collective understanding, or representational state, of the system, which in turn supports the cognitive activities the system performs. Collective understanding is also developed and changed, not just transmitted, through knowledge propagation. Knowledge is propagated via 'communicative pathways' such as speech, non-verbal communication, transformation of information by various modes, switching between modes of operation, and construction of new representations using both individual cognition and information contained in the technology.

One of the interesting consequences of the distributed cognition approach is the perspective it gives to understanding errors. Chapter 5 described approaches to error at work from the point of view of the individual, and how individuals may commit unsafe acts through using normal cognitive processes, and through deliberate safety violations. System errors were accounted for by viewing the interaction of unsafe acts with latent errors in the system and organisational context. Distributed cognition provides another insight into the process. Breakdowns in the functional system can occur as a result of situations where access to shared knowledge is disrupted, or a mismatch between shared expectations arises. These situations, if undetected, could lead to inappropriate actions, or critical actions not being carried out at the appropriate time.

To understand how breakdowns occur, or what newly designed technology would be required to do, it is necessary to focus on the dynamic aspects of activity in some detail. An example of the kinds of information gained by the approach is illustrated by Yvonne Rogers and Judy Ellis in a study of a hospital radiology department, whose function is largely to take X-rays of patients. The hospital wanted to introduce a hospital-wide computer system for the recording and transmission of information on patients and work-flow. The system would replace the existing department-specific ones.

In the radiology department, a particular interest was in the request form. Officially this had three main functions: to convey a request for examination; to transmit sufficient information about patients so that the appropriate examination could take place; and to record the results of the examination. In practice researchers found that the main purpose of the form was to give 'permission' for the examination. Information about the patient often was fragmentary, and further information had to be sought by staff; and results of the examination were often omitted from the form.

One particular part of the radiography department, called the Mobile Unit, provided an X-ray service to those in the hospital unable to come to the department. The Mobile Unit consisted of radiographers who rotated in and out of the unit on a monthly basis; the only permanent member of staff was the unit manager. For the Mobile Unit the request form was usually only seen at the point of contact with the patient. Thus the form was not a request for service, but was very definitely a 'permission'. No form meant no service. The request for service was usually telephoned through to the unit. A brief synopsis of the telephone message, rather than the form, often served as the basis for important decisions such as prioritisation of attendance, selection of the radiographer, provision of the correct number of X-rays, which ward or operating theatre the patient was in, the type of examination required, and the time at which the request was received. The decisions were affected by other needs arising from other requests, or anticipated requests, by individual preferences and expertise.

In order to co-ordinate the activities of the unit, information on requests, staff currently working on requests, and equipment locations at any particular time was needed so that individual staff members returning from a request could decide about the next one. The information needed was displayed on charts near incoming requests. In addition to the charts, the radiography department had a specialised computer system for patient details, although this was used by the Mobile Unit only after an examination had been completed.

The new hospital-wide computer system would need to be designed to take into account the information and activities needed to work effectively. A system which did not capture the richness of current practices would have a critical impact on the efficiency of the group, on the understanding of the current status of activities by staff, and on the anticipation of potential breakdowns in the delivery of X-ray services to patients. In short, information cannot be regarded solely in terms of facts about patients.

From the distributed cognition perspective the focus is on the way in which groups and technology interact in the work setting, and analysis must therefore concentrate on the way in which technology is used to support working practices.

Social aspects of working in groups

Merely putting people into work teams and setting them to work is not a guarantee of success. Research on group functioning and decision-making has highlighted several difficulties connected to group work.

Group development

All groups, regardless of roles, have certain rules or 'norms' governing a variety of things such as working practices, conduct and dress. Norms can develop through group leaders or dominant members, from group history and past situations. Group processes such as conformity help maintain norms. Conflict, on the other hand, can divide a group unless resolved. Group cohesiveness is important for effective group work. Tuckman (1965) identified four main stages in group development from a social and emotional point of view: forming, storming, norming and performing. Forming is the initial coming together of group members and the identification of the group's purpose, composition and terms of reference. Storming is the stage at which views are openly expressed about the nature of the tasks and arrangement of the group. This stage can lead to conflict and hostility, but can also give rise to discussion on the way forward. The next stage, norming, is then about establishing agreed procedures and standards. Finally, when the group has been through the first three stages, it can concentrate on the attainment of its purpose.

Groups and decision-making

The idea of groups at work is that they can be the means for different talents to meet and solve work-related problems. An example is the brainstorming meeting, which is designed to facilitate the generation of creative ideas (Osborn, 1957). A brainstorming session has a few basic rules, namely that no idea is too wacky; that criticism of ideas is not allowed; the more ideas the better, the quality is not important; and that members should try to build on others' ideas. Unfortunately, subsequent research has tended to show that brainstorming is not any better than individual idea creation (Diehl and Stroebe, 1987). Often the quantity of ideas produced by individuals working separately overtakes that of those working as a group. Research has compared the results achieved by actual groups made up of five people, with the aggregate of ideas produced by five people working alone, in an allotted time of five minutes. Actual groups produced an average of 37 ideas compared to 68 for the aggregate of those working on their own. Subsequent research has identified as a cause for the discrepancy the fact that in groups when one person is speaking others cannot voice their ideas. Waiting to speak means having less time to generate new ideas.

Interestingly, Rogelberg *et al.* (1992) observe that groups make better decisions than the average of decisions made by individual members. However, groups consistently make less good decisions than do the most able individuals in them. A variety of factors can contribute to this observation. West (1996) cites personality factors such as shyness and egocentricity. Shy group members may cause important information and opinions to be withheld, or not delivered with any impact, whereas egocentricity may mean that ideas are not listened to or considered properly. Social factors such as conformity may mean that opinions counter to the majority view are not voiced. Other social factors involve domination by particular individuals who hog the limelight, and the downgrading of some contributions because of the status or gender of the participant, thereby preventing proper discussion of other perspectives. Group members may lack effective communication skills.

Processes that can affect the decisions taken by any group, not just brainstormers, are **groupthink** and **risky shift**. Groupthink is where, in rare circumstances, critical evaluation of ideas is suspended and decisions are arrived at without proper consideration. Risky shift is where decisions become more extreme than any individual in the group would make, and the tendency noted in initial studies was for riskier decisions. Later research showed that groups can also show a cautious shift. Thus group decisions have the propensity to be more extreme, in either direction, than those of any one individual member.

Team-working and performance

Several factors have been identified as important to effective group performance. Weldon and Weingart (1994) reviewed over 30 studies of group performance across a range of tasks in the manufacturing and service sectors, such as harvesting, operating a restaurant and opening mail. The common theme was that the setting of group goals helped performance and productivity. In particular, specifying goals and the setting of difficult goals were found to improve group performance in contrast to vague and easy-to-attain goals. Commitment to group goals was linked, unsurprisingly, to the likelihood of attaining them. Other factors found to be relevant to commitment were the compatibility of personal goals to the group goals, having a charismatic leader, and expectations that the group goals can be achieved successfully.

Group functioning can be less effective than the aggregate of individual efforts. Group processes which hamper realisation of full group functioning have been called 'process losses' (Steiner, 1972). One such process loss which has received attention is 'social loafing'. Social loafing is where individuals work less hard when their efforts are combined with others' than when they are individually accountable (George, 1992).

In order to combat social loafing, Guzzo and Shea (1992) suggested that individuals should feel that they are important to how the group performs. Individual roles should be meaningful and intrinsically rewarding, and individual contributions should be visible and evaluated.

Weldon and Weingart (1994) put forward five ways in which group work can be supported. First, goals should be specified for all aspects of performance that relates to the effectiveness of the group. Second, feedback should be provided about progress. Third, interaction between the group members should be facilitated by removing physical barriers as far as possible. Fourth, ways in which individual contributions can be identified and co-ordinated should be considered, and fifth, management of failure should be facilitated.

Leadership and group-working

Leadership is the ability to direct a group to the attainment of goals. At work a leader may be a manager, company chairman or some other powerful person, but could instead be a person with no official status such as a work group member. Thus management and leadership are usually considered as separate in occupational psychology. Leadership has been studied from three perspectives: the personal characteristics of leaders; leadership behaviour; and the interaction between characteristics and work situations.

Early theories of leadership suggested that specific personality traits such as courage, foresight, intelligence, persuasiveness and charisma were associated with effective leaders. The usual way of trying to identify the necessary traits was to examine the background of leaders. The approach of course ignores environmental factors in the emergence of leaders, and the possibility that others with the same traits did not become leaders. Mann (1959) found little evidence for any individual trait being associated with leadership. However, that is probably not the end of the story since some common characteristics between leaders have been adduced by Bass (1981). Leaders were reported to have high energy levels, good judgement, good communication skills, assertiveness, the ability to co-operate and tactfulness to their followers.

Another tactic adopted by some researchers at Ohio State University was to study leadership behaviour. The behaviours thus observed could be clustered into two dimensions: initiating structure and consideration. Initiating structure is about tasks and getting the job done efficiently and on time. Consideration is about worker welfare and development. Worker satisfaction has been found to be higher when managers were high on consideration (Morse and Reimer, 1956), but the two dimensions have been found not to be consistently related to productivity (Stogdill, 1965).

Fiedler (1967) has proposed that leadership is effective when the leader's management style fits with the degree to which the work situation gives control and influence to the leader. Favourable situations incorporate a liking of the leader, well-defined tasks and high leader power. Structure-oriented leaders do better in high- or low-control situations, whereas consideration-oriented leaders do better in moderate-control situations.

Subsequent research has tended to lend support to Fiedler's hypothesis, although not all studies have confirmed it (Strube and Garcia, 1981). Fiedler went on to suggest that leadership style could not be changed as easily as the organisation, and therefore change to the organisation could help leaders, for example by making tasks more defined.

Recently the emphasis has tended towards there being no one best style of leadership. Rodrigues (1988) has suggested that three types of leader are needed for organisations which exist in a dynamic environment. The 'innovator' is characterised by the search for new ideas, boldness, the will to succeed, and the belief that the environment can be controlled and manipulated. This style is likely to be effective when an organisation is setting up or renewing. The 'implementer' is typified by the ability to accomplish goals through people, a systematic approach, a willingness to take responsibility for decisions, and the need to control and influence situations. This style is likely to be most effective at the stage where new ideas are consolidated. Finally, the 'pacifier' is characterised by the capacity to decentralise decision-making, an ability to pacify important individuals, a desire to use earlier decisions, and the need for a positive social interaction in the workplace. This style is likely to be effective when a stable work environment has been implemented, and people in the organisation feel competent to do the job.

Work groups

Work groups can be defined as consisting of two or more people engaged together in meeting a goal or set of goals. The groups can be formal, such as management teams, the quality circles common in Japanese industry, or the autonomous work groups in European firms, or informal. Quality circles, popular in Japan and now the USA, are small groups of employees from the same work areas who meet regularly to identify, analyse and solve quality and other work problems. Circle members are trained in quality control, develop communication skills and learn problem-solving techniques.

Within groups individuals can have different roles, and hold role expectations about their responsibilities. Benne and Sheats (1948) outlined a number of roles under three headings: group task roles; group building and maintenance roles; and self-centred roles. Group task roles included that of initiator/contributor – a person who recommends new ideas about a problem; information-giver – a person who contributes relevant information to help with decision-making; and elaborator – a person who expands on the points made by others. Examples of group building roles were encourager, harmoniser, compromiser, follower. Self-centred roles included aggressor – a person who tries to promote his or her own status in the group; blocker – a person who attempts to stymie group action; playboy – a person who engages in humour and irrelevant acts to divert the group focus away from the tasks in hand; and help-seeker – a person who tries to gain sympathy by expressing insecurity or inadequacy.

A more recent exposition of roles in management teams has been proposed by Belbin (1981). He suggested eight roles useful to have in teams: shaper; resource investigator; monitor–evaluator; completer–finisher; team-worker; plant (individualistic, but creative); chairman; and company worker. The basic idea behind these roles is that an effective team is made up of different roles so the whole is greater than the sum of the parts, and some support for this view has been recently reported (Senior, 1997).

An alternative perspective to looking at group roles is to consider group composition. This refers to how similar or dissimilar group members are, in terms of age, sex, educational attainment, training, ability level, attitudes and values, as well as personality. Research has shown that groups made up of people with varied professional backgrounds appear to produce more creative decisions of a higher quality than do professionally homogeneous groups. In contrast, group cohesiveness is associated with members of a group who have similar demographic backgrounds; that is, they are similar in terms of age, sex and educational attainment. Demographic similarity also predicts how long a group is likely to stay as a group.

Group cohesiveness has been found to be associated with the performance of the group in high-performance work teams (Mullen and Copper, 1994). However, the association was not very strong. Interestingly, there was a stronger association from performance to cohesiveness than vice versa. Thus it would seem more beneficial to help teams work effectively together than to build team cohesiveness in the hope that better performance will follow. For example, clarifying goals and identifying individual contributions may be a better approach to team-building than interventions designed to increase members' liking for each other.

Defining and measuring group performance is not always easy. For example, group effectiveness could be considered in terms of three types of outcome: meeting organisational goals; the length of time for which the group continues to function; and the effects on the mental health and development of team members (West, 1996). Obviously work teams must meet organisational goals to be considered effective and worth instituting formally in the workplace. One aspect of organisational functioning, at least in some sectors of the economy, is the ability to innovate and develop new ways of doing things which benefit the organisation and the people whose needs it meets. West and Anderson (1993) studied hospital management teams and found that innovativeness, as rated by external experts, was inversely related to the size of the team and the resources available to it. It was observed that individual commitment to goals, information sharing, influence over decision-making and interaction with other team members were positively associated with innovativeness. Practical support for innovation, constructive controversy and monitoring performance also predicted innovativeness in teams.

Team viability, or the team members' satisfaction, participation and willingness to continue to work together, has been observed to relate to four social dimensions (West, 1994). The dimensions are social support within the team, the effectiveness of ways of resolving conflict between team members, the social climate of the team and the support for the growth and development of team members.

Campion *et al.* (1993) investigated the relationship between characteristics of work groups and their effectiveness in a financial organisation. They measured effectiveness by productivity, employee satisfaction and the judgements of managers. Campion *et al.* identified five groupings for the team characteristics they studied:

- job design (at the team level), which included team self-management, participation, task variety, task significance and task identity;
- interdependence (between team members), which included task interdependence, goal interdependence and interdependence of feedback and rewards;
- composition (of the team), which included heterogeneity, flexibility, relative size and preference for group work;
- context (resources the group receives from the organisation), which included training, managerial support and communication and co-operation between groups;
- process (the way in which members of the team interact), which included potency (the extent to which team members believe they can be effective), social support, workload sharing and communication and co-operation within groups.

They collected data from over 450 workers (391 employees and 70 managers) using a questionnaire asking for ratings on 54 items measuring the characteristics, and studied archival records of 80 work groups. The groups studied varied in size from six to 30 people, and five people plus the manager were asked to fill in the questionnaire from each group. Almost all the employees were female (96 per cent). The groups were involved in clerical work. Tasks included coding, computer input and answering customer queries.

Campion *et al.* (1993) found a significant association between all the effectiveness measures and all the five groupings of team work characteristics. At a more detailed level of analysis, the strongest associations were between job design aspects and effectiveness, and the process aspects and effectiveness. When individual characteristics were considered, rather than groupings, not all the 19 characteristics studied were associated with all the effectiveness measures. However, all bar two of the characteristics were associated with at least one of the effectiveness measures. The odd ones out were task identity (a job design characteristic) and communication and co-operation between groups (a context characteristic). Task identity is the extent to which a group completes a whole and separate piece of work. It is a puzzle that this characteristic was not associated with effectiveness as it was emphasised from socio-technical systems theory to be important for optimising the socio-technical system. However, Campion *et al.* note certain limitations in their study which could explain the lack of association between characteristics and effectiveness. Principal among them is that the analysis was at the group level, which meant that the power of the statistical tests used was 'only moderate'. A second suggestion was that the measures themselves could be further refined to be more sensitive.

So far in this chapter the outline of various approaches to group work and technology has tended to reflect the fact that research has adopted different psychological perspectives, either cognitive, social or organisational. The understanding of cognitive, social and organisational aspects of team-working and technology is still growing. The difference in the frameworks adopted makes it difficult to relate them to each other easily. One approach is to focus on the knowledge, skills and abilities needed for successful team work, rather than on personality types. In this way the tasks associated with new technology could be analysed in similar terms. Stevens and Campion (1994) have reviewed group-working from the point of view of the knowledge, skills and abilities needed for successful teamwork. Their concern was the human resource management issues connected to team-working, but their focus was away from personality traits and towards knowledge, skills and abilities (KSAs), and addressed to the individual rather than team level of analysis. They identified 14 KSAs, grouped under two broad headings: interpersonal KSAs and self-management KSAs. Interpersonal KSAs came under the headings of conflict resolution, collaborative problem-solving and communication KSAs, and self-management KSAs came under the headings of goal setting and performance management, and planning and task co-ordination KSAs. Clearly, Stevens and Campion's account is a typology of KSAs needed, in descriptive terms related to activities needed for good team-working, rather than a psychological analysis. Nonetheless, it may afford subsequent research into the psychological factors which support their analysis.

Summary

This chapter has considered team-working and technology from three points of view: cognitive, social and organisational psychology. The perspectives provided by these different points of view are, at present, relatively unintegrated. This is not surprising, given the different investigative traditions and concerns involved. It is also the case that much more research is needed before the issues involved in team-working and technology are fully understood. Nonetheless, it is possible to identify and discuss several important aspects. The first is that the socio-technical systems approach places emphasis on the joint optimisation of the social and technical parts of a system. The design tenets of such a system were discussed at the beginning of the chapter. Second, we have seen that cognitive approaches based not on traditional cognitive psychology but on distributed cognition offer promising insights relevant to working with technology in workplace settings. Third, that research into the social aspects of working in groups has produced a number of findings which provide an account of the barriers to working with other people in groups. Finally, the chapter discussed findings from groups operating in the workplace and highlighted several of the characteristics shown to be related to effectiveness.

Chapter 7

Concluding remarks

WORK WITH MODERN technology throws the spotlight on mental, rather than physical, skills and abilities. This book has concentrated on discussing psychological issues related to jobs and technology, and the link between them. The book focuses on topic areas and theories which are mainstream in what could be called 'fitting the person to the job and technology, and the job and technology to the person'. The emphasis is on attitudes, perceptions and mental capabilities in relation to technology and work.

A key feature of the book is that the discussion of individual mental processing is set within, and linked to, the job level of analysis, rather than being restricted to the task level. Jobs entail carrying out several tasks, often with other people, in an organisational setting. For example, chemical process operators work in teams to control the manufacture of chemical compounds through computer consoles, which requires an understanding of the process, and of how control actions affect the safety, quality and cost of the product. Within a team the operators can talk to each other because they sit side by side. However, if they want to communicate with other operators in other parts of the factory they may well use electronic mail, requiring a different type of knowledge and style of communication. Thus the relationship of equipment and system design and use to psychological factors cannot be understood without reference to more organisational aspects of work.

What the book is not about is organisational psychology *per se*. It is important to realise that there is much more written on management and organisational psychology than is mentioned here. The purpose of the book was to introduce important topics to those without previous knowledge of them, and to illustrate the relevance of psychological knowledge to the analysis of jobs and use of technology.

Whichever way organisations arrange themselves, jobs and tasks will still be there to be done, and the psychology involved with technology will be part of how effective the use of new technology is. How far have we come, then, and what is there still to do? The following discusses some of the main points.

The psychology involved with technology encompasses aspects of social, cognitive and organisational processes, at least. Important advances in understanding have been made in all these fields. It can be stated with some confidence that job control is important to feelings of psychological strain, and to the benefits of learning about technology through hands-on experience. Now, the nature of human limitations in mental information processing is much clearer, and the implications for the design of work environments, jobs and tasks more apparent. Frameworks for considering the contributions of cognitive and social processes to working safely with complex technological systems have been developed, and an agenda for research on socio-technical systems through approaches such as distributed cognition sketched out.

Chapter 2 outlined the main approaches to job design, job and task analysis, job satisfaction and job-related stress. Job design is concerned with aspects of jobs which are applicable, in principle, to a broad range of jobs. Research has identified several characteristics of jobs important for psychological well-being. Autonomy has emerged as a crucial aspect of jobs. The relationship of job design to performance is less well understood. There are suggestions concerning what affects the relationship, but further work is needed before a more complete picture emerges. Recent developments in manufacturing have placed greater emphasis on employee flexibility and job-related knowledge. Other aspects of jobs, which have not yet been fully explored, may turn out to be important.

A potential casualty of increasing employee flexibility could be job analysis itself. Future working patterns may mean that the content of jobs and the abilities required to do them will change over relatively short time scales. However, jobs will always consist of tasks, and thus task analysis, concerned with the detailed nature of tasks and their sequencing, should remain important.

Chapter 3 considered the main personnel functions related to the demands of new technology. The aim of personnel functions is to match people to tasks and jobs. Technology, especially computer-controlled technology, has meant that the skills required are more mental than manual, and thus a premium is placed on cognitive skill acquisition and the training of mental skills and problem-solving techniques. Research on skill with work technology has more questions to answer. For example, do different types of work system require different types of knowledge, and learning conditions, and what are the implications for training programmes? Changes in technology and markets imply a commitment to life-long learning, and raise awkward questions about how personnel functions will support it, and adapt with it.

Chapter 4 considered the relationship between technology and people from the point of view of the person as a processor of information, and the technology as imposing mental, rather than physical, demands on the person. Mental workload was discussed, and theories about mental capacity were outlined in terms of processing resources and informational limits. Thereafter variability in mental processing efficiency was considered, especially in terms of aspects of the environment, changes in the state of the individual, and as a function of time of day and circadian rhythms. All the aspects considered have implications for work system and equipment design. However, many of the tasks studied have been perceptual–motor tasks rather than cognitive ones, studied in the laboratory. Where more 'intellectual' tasks have been considered they have often consisted of rather simple problem-solving activities. Thus there is a question of what the relationship is between the views gained from relatively simple and discrete tasks, and more complex, continuous and interactive tasks, and between laboratory tasks and those actually performed at work.

Chapter 5 sought to outline the main psychological approaches to safety in work settings, with an emphasis on technological work systems. Psychological approaches to safety at work have been informed by cognitive and social psychology. Human error was discussed in terms of its relationship to cognitive processing of information. Violations of safety procedures were discussed in relation to perceptions and attitudes towards hazards and safety from a social psychology perspective. The framework and taxonomy presented demonstrated the power and fecundity of basing an analysis on the individual, and its relation to unsafe acts. However, organisational aspects were shown to be important too. Organisational and systems approaches to safety discussed how organisational climate influences safety behaviour, and how error analyses could explain technological systems disasters. However, the psychology of how individual and organisational aspects of safety are linked is not well understood, and will need more research. The nascent approach of distributed cognition, discussed in Chapter 6, may well turn out to have a significant contribution to make.

Chapter 6 considered team-working and technology from three points of view: cognitive, social and organisational psychology. The perspectives provided by these different points of view are, at present, relatively unintegrated. The socio-technical systems approach places emphasis on the joint optimisation of the social and technical parts of a system, with consequences for system design. However, it is still the case that the social part of the system tends to get organised round the technology. The chapter discussed computer-supported co-operative work and distributed cognition. The latter, particularly, promises new insights relevant to working with technology in workplace settings, but at the moment is in its infancy. The field is ripe for further research effort in work settings, with all the advantages that brings in terms of the richness and 'real-world' nature of the processes studied. Key questions are: what should the technology provide users so they understand the work system, and the other people using it for common goals? How do work teams break down, or work more or less efficiently, as a function of distributed knowledge, technological artefacts, personality and other differences between team members? Excitingly, distributed cognition offers the potential to understand co-operative work based on 'virtual' organisations, where those working together are in contact with each other only via computer, for example, and workers could be based almost anywhere. The social implications of this new way of working have only just begun to be explored.

Current knowledge is still limited in face of the challenge posed by the very latest technological advances in computers. The challenge resides in the fact that computers provide for the opportunity to design and implement integrated command, control and information systems, and for these systems to support very flexible ways of working and communicating. The crucial issue integration raises is how the various psychological aspects – social, cognitive and organisational – interact with each other and wider organisational concerns. Future research will shed some light on this and other questions arising out of people doing jobs with technology.

Glossary

The first occurrence of each of these terms is highlighted in **bold** type in the main text.

ability tests Tests which measure competencies, such as deductive reasoning.

accident proneness The now discredited idea that particular people are more liable to have an accident.

advanced manufacturing technology (AMT) Computer-controlled machines and robots used to produce finished products.

antecedent behaviour Behaviour leading up to an event (e.g. an accident).

assembly line Manufacturing method where a product is assembled in sequence by different employees.

automation The performance by technology of what had previously been human functions.

burnout Job-related emotional exhaustion leading to less engagement with the job.

circadian rhythms Fluctuations in human functions over 24 hours (e.g. body temperature).

cognitive failure Temporary breakdown in basic mental processing of information.

cognitive psychology Branch of psychology which studies mental processes and mechanisms.

cognitive task Activity which demands higher mental processes such as decision-making.

compensatory effort An attempt to maintain task performance under stressful conditions by putting in more mental effort.

declarative knowledge Knowledge of facts which can be verbalised, knowing that . . .

distributed cognition Approach to understanding how technology and teams work to meet functional goals. Communication, knowledge and the artefacts used are central concerns.

EEG recordings Records of the electrical activity of the brain.

ergonomics Study of the person in relation to their working environment.

extrinsic job satisfaction Satisfaction related to the context of a job, such as pay, rather than the job itself.

groupthink Phenomenon in group decision-making where conclusions are formed without proper consideration.

Hawthorne effect The influence on productivity of interest being shown in workers by researchers and management.

heart rate variability Fluctuations in the inter-beat interval of the heart.

human error Area of study emphasising that cognitive mistakes, slips and lapses in people are related to normal mental processes.

information processing approach Psychological perspective on mental activity which uses a metaphor of the mind as a processor of information.

intrinsic job satisfaction Satisfaction related to the job itself, for example the variety of activities in a job.

job analysis Process whereby the responsibilities and tasks that constitute a job are identified.

job design Area of enquiry in occupational psychology which is concerned with the nature of jobs and their effect on work performance and well-being.

job simplification The restriction of workers to a narrow range of standardised tasks. The responsibility for how tasks are organised and carried out is vested in management.

just in time (JIT) In manufacturing, techniques which relate customer orders to the amount of raw materials needed so that the stock of raw and partially finished materials is minimised.

management by objectives (MBO) Process whereby work performance goals are set, against which employees can be appraised.

mental capabilities Fundamental functions of the mind, and their limitations, such as memory, attention and thinking.

microelectronics Generic name for technology using miniature solid-state electronic devices such as transistors and microchips.

perceptual–motor task Activity requiring a speeded response to sensory information.

physiological measures Measures of bodily activity, e.g. galvanic skin response (GSR) to measure perspiration.

primary task The task given priority when doing two or more tasks together.

procedural knowledge Knowledge about how to do something, knowing how …

reliability (of a test or measure) The ability of a test consistently to measure the same thing every time it is used.

risky shift Phenomenon in group decision-making where group conclusions are more extreme than those of any individual.

safety climate The shared perceptions by workers about an organisation's approach to safety.

scientific management The view that work should be broken down into standardised, simple tasks done in the most efficient way possible. Also called Taylorism, after Frederick W. Taylor, who espoused it.

secondary task The task given the lower priority in performance terms when doing two tasks together.

serial reaction or **responding** Perceptual–motor task requiring continuous responding for the duration of the task.

shiftwork Work schedules which entail working outside normal working hours (e.g. at night).

social loafing The tendency of some individuals to work less hard when working with others in a team.

socio-technical systems theory View that both social and technological parts of a work system should be jointly optimised.

supervisory control A common form of control of technology, where the technology performs most of the work and the operator merely monitors progress, and intervenes only in an emergency.

task allocation The process and result of deciding which work tasks to give to the person and which to the technology.

task analysis Process whereby the sequencing and timing of activities, and the mental operations needed to perform a task, are identified.

total quality management (TQM) In manufacturing, an integrated approach to embodying quality in the manufacturing process, rather than having quality control after the product has been made.

validity (of a test or measure) The ability of a test to measure what it is supposed to. For example, to be valid an IQ test must succeed in measuring intelligence.

verbal protocols What people say they are or were doing and thinking when engaged in task activity, recorded under systematic conditions.

working memory The memory involved in enabling mental activity; for example, mental arithmetic needs mental storage space to hold calculations in mind until they are finished.

Annotated further reading

In contrast to other books in the Psychology Focus series, the readings below are given only at the end of the book, rather than at the end of each chapter. There are a number of reasons for this difference. The primary reason is that *Jobs, Technology and People* attempts to integrate findings from a number of disparate psychological areas: cognitive, social and organisational. The suggested readings therefore are chosen to provide more information across these areas related to the concerns in the present book. The reader is urged to look at these readings, and the chapters within them, with a selective eye initially, but then to branch out into other chapters which appear interesting. To help this process I have indicated the chapters in *Jobs, Technology and People* next to the reading I judge most applicable. However, most of the readings below apply to some degree to all the chapters in the present book.

Arnold, J., Cooper, C. and Robertson, I. (1995) *Work Psychology*, 2nd edition, London:

Pitman. (Most relevant to Chapters 2 and 3.) A basic, readable introduction to a range of work psychology issues, especially personnel work.

Holloway, W. (1991) *Work Psychology and Organisational Behaviour*, London: Sage. (Most relevant to Chapters 1 and 2.) An interesting interpretation of the history of work psychology.

Robson, C. (1993) *Real World Research*, Oxford: Blackwell. (Most relevant to Chapter 1.) A readable, although somewhat long, account of the various approaches to studying people in real-life situations. The book details many of the theoretical issues that need to be thought about before carrying out investigations of psychology in the workplace.

Warr, P. (ed.) (1996) *Psychology at Work*, 4th edition, London: Penguin. (Most relevant to Chapters 2, 3, 4 and 6.) This book contains a selection of topics on issues relevant to the workplace, drawn from across the range of work psychology. Each topic is the subject of a chapter written by a different author. Some chapters are more relevant than others to *Jobs, Technology and People*, but the book provides the opportunity to read more widely around work psychology.

Wickens, C.D. (1992) *Engineering Psychology and Human Performance*, 2nd edition, New York: HarperCollins. (Most relevant to Chapters 4 and 5.) This book provides an excellent discussion of human information processing, and how it works in a large number of perceptual–motor and cognitive tasks relevant to work and the use of technology. The book is not an easy read without some background in cognitive psychology.

References

Adams, J.S. (1965) 'Inequity in social exchange', in L. Berkowitz (ed.) *Advances in Experimental Social Psychology*, vol. 2, New York: Academic Press.

Allport, D., Antonis, B. and Reynolds, P. (1972) 'On the division of attention: a disproof of the single channel hypothesis', *Quarterly Journal of Experimental Psychology*, 24, 225–235.

Anderson, J. (1982) 'Acquisition of cognitive skill', *Psychological Review*, 89, 396–406.

Anderson, J. (1983) *The Architecture of Cognition*, Cambridge, MA: Harvard University Press.

Anderson, J. (1987) 'Skill acquisition: compilation of weak-method problem solutions', *Psychological Review*, 94, 192–210.

Anderson, J. (1995) *Cognitive Psychology and its Implications*, 4th edition, New York: Freeman.

Anderson, N. and Shackleton, V. (1993) *Successful Selection Interviewing*, Oxford: Blackwell.

145

REFERENCES

Annett, J. and Duncan, K. (1967) 'Task analysis and training design', *Occupational Psychology*, 41, 211–221.

Bandura, A. (1977) *Social Learning Theory*, Englewood Cliffs, NJ: Prentice-Hall.

Banks, M. (1988) 'Jobs components inventory', in S. Gael (ed.) *Job Analysis Handbook*, New York: Wiley.

Barrett, G.V. (1992) 'Clarifying construct validity: definitions, processes, and models', *Human Performance*, 5, 13–58.

Bartlett, F. (1932) *Remembering*, Cambridge: Cambridge University Press.

Bass, B.M. (1981) *Stogdill's Handbook of Leadership*, New York: Free Press.

Beehr, T.A. and Bhagat, R.S. (eds) (1985) *Human Stress and Cognition in Organizations: An Integrated Perspective*, New York: Wiley.

Belbin, R.M. (1981) *Management Teams: Why They Succeed or Fail*, Oxford: Butterworth Heinemann.

Benne, K.D. and Sheats, P. (1948) 'Functional roles of group members', *Journal of Social Issues*, 4, 41–49.

Berry, D. (1991) 'The role of action in implicit learning', *Quarterly Journal of Experimental Psychology*, 43A, 881–906.

Blanz, F. and Ghiselli, E.E. (1972) 'The mixed standard scale: a new rating system', *Personnel Psychology*, 25, 185–199.

Braverman, H. (1974) *Labour and Monopoly Capital: The Degradation of Work in the Twentieth Century*, New York: Monthly Review Press.

Broadbent, D. (1954) 'Some effects of noise on visual performance', *Quarterly Journal of Experimental Psychology*, 6, 1–5.

Broadbent, D. (1958) *Perception and Communication*, Oxford: Pergamon Press.

Broadbent, D. (1979) 'Is a fatigue test now possible?', *Ergonomics*, 22, 1277–1290.

Broadbent, D. (1982) 'Task combination and the selective intake of information', *Acta Psychologia*, 50, 253–290.

Broadbent, D. (1990) 'Effective decisions and their verbal justification', in D.E. Broadbent, A. Baddeley and J. Reason (eds) *Human Factors in Hazardous Situations*, Oxford: Oxford Scientific Publications.

Brown, I. (1990) 'Accident reporting and analysis', in J. Wilson and N. Corlett (eds) *Evaluation of Human Work*, London: Taylor & Francis.

Butler, M.C. and Jones, A.P. (1979) 'Perceived leader behavior, individual characteristics, and injury occurrence in hazardous work environments', *Journal of Applied Psychology*, 64, 299–304.

Campbell, S. (1992) 'Effects of sleep and circadian rhythms on performance', in A.P. Smith and D. Jones (eds) *Handbook of Human Performance*, vol. 3, New York: Academic Press.

Campion, J.E. (1972) 'Work sampling for personnel selection', *Journal of Applied Psychology*, 56, 40–44.

Campion, M., Medsker, G. and Higgs, A. (1993) 'Relations between work group characteristics and effectiveness: implications for designing effective work groups', *Personnel Psychology*, 46, 823–850.

Charuwatee, P. (1996) 'An investigation of perceived organizational safety climate: employees' intentions to behave safely and their predictors', unpublished MSc thesis, University of Sheffield, UK.

Cherns, A. (1976) 'The principles of sociotechnical design', *Human Relations*, 29, 783–792.

Chi, M., Glaser, R. and Farr, M. (eds) (1988) *The Nature of Expertise*, Hillsdale, NJ: Erlbaum.

Chmiel, N. and Wall, T. (1994) 'Fault prevention, job design and the adaptive control of advanced manufacturing technology', *Applied Psychology: An International Review*, 43 (4), 455–473.

Chmiel, N., Totterdell, P. and Folkard, S. (1995) 'On adaptive control, sleep loss and fatigue', *Applied Cognitive Psychology*, 9, S39–S53.

Clegg, C.W. (1983) 'Psychology of employee lateness, absence, and turnover: a methodological critique', *Journal of Applied Psychology*, 68, 88–101.

Clegg, C.W. and Corbett, J.M. (1986) 'Psychological and organisational aspects of computer aided manufacturing', *Current Psychological Research and Reviews*, 5, 189–204.

Cook, M. (1993) *Personnel Selection and Productivity*, 2nd edition, Chichester: Wiley.

Cooper, C., Cooper, R. and Eaker, L. (1988) *Living with Stress*, London: Penguin.

Cordes, C. and Dougherty, T. (1993) 'A review and integration of research on job burnout', *Academy of Management Review*, 18, 621–656.

Cox, S. and Cox, T. (1991) 'The structure of employees' attitudes to safety: a European example', *Work and Stress*, 5, 93–106.

Craig, A. and Cooper, R. (1992) 'Symptoms of acute and chronic fatigue', in A.P. Smith and D. Jones (eds) *Handbook of Human Performance*, vol. 3, New York: Academic Press.

Crossman, E. (1959) 'A theory of the acquisition of speed-skill', *Ergonomics*, 2, 153–166.

Davis, L., Canter, R. and Hoffman, J. (1955) 'Current job design criteria', *Journal of Industrial Engineering*, 6, 5–11.

Dean, J.W. and Snell, S.A. (1991) 'Integrated manufacturing and job design: moderating effects of organizational inertia', *Academy of Management Journal*, 34, 774–804.

Dedobbeleer, N. and Beland, F. (1991) 'A safety climate measure for construction sites', *Journal of Safety Research*, 22, 97–103.

Dejoy, D. (1986) 'A behavioural-diagnostic model for self-protective behaviour in the workplace', *Professional Safety*, 31, 26–30.

Diehl, M. and Stroebe, W. (1987) 'Productivity loss in brainstorming groups: toward the solution of a riddle', *Journal of Personality and Social Psychology*, 53, 497–509.

Dienstbier, R. (1989) 'Arousal and physiological toughness: implications for mental and physical health', *Psychological Review*, 96, 84–100.

Drucker, P.F. (1954) *The Practice of Management*, New York: Harper & Row.

Duncan, K. (1972) 'Strategies for the analysis of the task', in T. Hartley (ed.) *Strategies for Programmed Instruction and Educational Technology*, London: Butterworth.

Edwards, J. (1992) 'A cybernetic theory of stress, coping and well-being in organizations', *Academy of Management Review*, 17, 238–274.

Elkin, A. and Rosch, P. (1990) 'Promoting mental health in the workplace: the prevention side of stress management', *Occupational Medicine: State of the Art Review*, 5, 739–754.

Ettlie, J. (1986) 'Facing the factory of the future', in D.D. Davis (ed.) *Managing Technical Innovation*, San Francisco: Jossey-Bass.

Fanger, P.O. (1970) *Thermal Comfort, Analysis, and Applications in Environmental Engineering*, Copenhagen: Danish Technical Press.

Fiedler, F.E. (1967) *A Theory of Leadership Effectiveness*, New York: McGraw-Hill.

Fitts, P. (1962) 'Factors in complex skill training', in R. Glaser (ed.) *Training Research and Education*, Pittsburgh: University of Pittsburgh.

Foley, P., Watts, D. and Wilson, B. (1993) 'New technologies, skills shortages and training strategies', in P. Swann (ed.) *New Technologies and the Firm: Innovation and Competition*, London: Routledge.

Folkard, S. (1983) 'Diurnal variation', in G.R. Hockey (ed.) *Stress and Fatigue in Human Performance*, Chichester: Wiley.

Folkard, S. (1996) 'Body rhythms and shiftwork', in P. Warr (ed.) *Psychology at Work*, London: Penguin.

Folkard, S. and Monk, T. (1979) 'Shiftwork and performance', *Human Factors*, 21, 483–492.

French, J., Caplan, R. and Harrison, V. (1982) *The Mechanisms of Job Stress and Strain*, Chichester: Wiley.

Frese, M. (1987) 'Human–computer interaction in the office', in C. Cooper and I. Robertson (eds) *International Review of Industrial and Organisational Psychology*, London: Wiley.

Frese, M. and Zapf, D. (1993) 'Action as the core of work psychology: a German approach', in M. Dunnette, I. Hough and H. Triandis (eds) *Handbook of Industrial and Organisational Psychology*, vol. 4, Palo Alto, CA: Consulting Psychologist Press.

Fried, Y. and Ferris, G.R. (1987) 'The validity of the job characteristics model: a review and meta-analysis', *Personnel Psychology*, 40, 287–322.

Friedman, M. and Rosenman, R.H. (1974) *Type A Behavior and Your Heart*, New York: Alfred A. Knopf.

Gardner, G. and Gould, L. (1989) 'Public perceptions of the risks and benefits of technology', *Risk Analysis*, 9, 225–242.

Gardner, P., Chmiel, N. and Wall, T. (1996) 'Implicit knowledge and fault diagnosis in the control of advanced manufacturing technology', *Behaviour and Information Technology*, 15, 205–212.

George, J. (1992) 'Extrinsic and intrinsic origins of perceived social loafing in organizations', *Academy of Management Journal*, 35, 191–202.

Goldberg, A., Dar-El, E. and Rubin, A. (1991) 'Threat perception and the readiness to participate in safety programs', *Journal of Organizational Behaviour*, 12, 109–122.

Greenberg, J. and Ornstein, S. (1983) 'High status job title as compensation for underpayment: a test of equity theory', *Journal of Applied Psychology*, 68, 285–297.

Guzzo, R. and Shea, G. (1992) 'Group performance and inter-group relations in organizations', in M. Dunnette, I. Hough and H. Triandis (eds) *Handbook of Industrial and Organisational Psychology*, vol. 3, Palo Alto, CA: Consulting Psychologist Press.

Hackman, J.R. (1983) 'The design of work teams', in J. Lorsch (ed.) *Handbook of Organizational Behaviour*, Englewood Cliffs, NJ: Prentice-Hall

Hackman, J.R. and Oldham, G.R. (1976) 'Motivation through the design of work: test of a theory', *Organizational Behavior and Human Performance*, 16, 250–279.

Hamilton, P., Hockey, G.R. and Rejman, M. (1977) 'The place of the concept of activation in human information theory: an integrative approach', in S. Dornic (ed.) *Attention and Performance VI*, New York: Academic Press.

Hancock, P.A. and Scallen, F.F. (1996) 'Allocating functions in human–machine systems', in R. Hoffman (ed.) *Psychology Beyond the Threshold: A Festschrift for William N. Dember*, New Jersey: Lawrence Erlbaum.

Haynes, R.S., Pine, R.C. and Fitch, H.G. (1982) 'Reducing accident rates with organizational behavior modification', *Academy of Management Journal*, 25, 407–416.

Herrick, N.Q. and Maccoby, M. (1975) 'Humanizing work: a priority goal of the 1970's', in L.E. Davis and A.B. Cherns (eds) *The Quality of Working Life*, vol. 1, New York: Free Press.

Herzberg, F. (1966) *Work and the Nature of Man*, Cleveland, OH: World.

Hick, W. (1952) 'On the rate of gain of information', *Quarterly Journal of Experimental Psychology*, 4, 11–26.

Hockey, G.R.J. (1970) 'Effects of loud noise on attentional selectivity', *Quarterly Journal of Experimental Psychology*, 22, 28–36.

Hockey, G.R.J. (1986) 'Changes in operator efficiency as a function of environmental stress, fatigue, and circadian rhythms', in K.R. Boff, L. Kaufman and J.P. Thomas (eds) *Handbook of Perception and Human Performance*, vol. 2, New York: Wiley.

Hockey, G.R.J. (1996) 'Skilled performance and mental workload', in P. Warr (ed.) *Psychology at Work*, London: Penguin.

Holding, D. (1983) 'Fatigue', in G.R. Hockey (ed.) *Stress and Fatigue in Human Performance*, Chichester: Wiley.

Holloway, W. (1991) *Work Psychology and Organisational Behaviour*, London: Sage.

Hutchins, E. (1995) *Cognition in the Wild*, Cambridge, MA: MIT Press.

Hyman, R. (1953) 'Stimulus information as a determinant of reaction time', *Journal of Experimental Psychology*, 45, 423–432.

Iaffaldano, M.T. and Muchinsky, P.M. (1985) 'Job satisfaction and job performance: a meta-analysis', *Psychological Bulletin*, 97, 251–273.

Jackson, P. and Wall, T. (1991) 'How does operator control enhance performance of advanced manufacturing technology?', *Ergonomics*, 34, 1301–1311.

Jackson, S.E., Schwab, R.L. and Schuler, R.S. (1986) 'Toward an understanding of the burnout phenomenon', *Journal of Applied Psychology*, 71, 630–640.

Jaikamur, R. (1986) 'Post industrial manufacturing', *Harvard Business Review*, 6, 69–76.

Johansen, R. (1988) *Groupware: Computer Support for Business Teams*, New York: The Free Press.

Jones, J. and Wuebker, L. (1985) 'Development and validation of the safety locus of control scale', *Perceptual and Motor Skills*, 61, 151–161.

Kahneman, D. (1973) *Attention and Effort*, Englewood Cliffs, NJ: Prentice-Hall.

Kahneman, D., Slovic, P. and Tversky, A. (eds) (1982) *Judgement Under Uncertainty: Heuristics and Biases*, Cambridge: Cambridge University Press.

Kantowitz, B. and Caspar, P. (1988) 'Human workload in aviation', in E. Weiner and D. Nagel (eds) *Human Factors in Aviation*, New York: Academic Press.

Karasek, R.A. (1979) 'Job demands, job decision latitude, and mental strain: implications for job redesign', *Administrative Science Quarterly*, 24, 285–307.

Kelly, J. (1982) *Scientific Management, Job Redesign and Work Performance*, London: Academic Press.

Kelly, J. (1992) 'Does job re-design theory explain job re-design outcomes?', *Human Relations*, 45, 753–774.

Kerr, W.A. (1950) 'Accident proneness of factory departments', *Journal of Applied Psychology*, 34, 167–170.

Kobrick, J.L. and Fine, B.J. (1983) 'Climate and human performance', in D.J. Oborne and M.M. Gruneberg (eds) *The Physical Environment at Work*, Chichester: Wiley.

Landy, F.J. (1976) 'The validity of the interview in police officer selection', *Journal of Applied Psychology*, 61, 193–198.

Landy, F.J. and Farr, J.L. (1980) 'Performance rating', *Psychological Bulletin*, 87, 72–107.

Latham, G.P., Steele, T.P. and Saari, L.M. (1982) 'The effects of participation and goal difficulty on performance', *Personnel Psychology*, 35, 677–686.

REFERENCES

Lazarus, R. and Folkman, S. (1984) *Stress, Appraisal and Coping*, New York: Springer.

Lundberg, U. and Frankenhaeuser, M. (1978) 'Psychophysiological reactions to noise as modified by personal control over noise intensity', *Biological Psychology*, 6, 55–59.

McClelland, D.C. (1961) *The Achieving Society*, New York: Van Nostrand.

McClelland, D.C. (1975) *Power: The Inner Experience*, New York: Irvington Press.

McClelland, D.C. (1988) *Human Motivation*, Cambridge: Cambridge University Press.

McConkey, D.D. (1983) *How to Manage by Results*, 4th edition, New York: AMACOM.

McCormick, E.J., Jeanneret, P.R. and Mecham, R.C. (1972) 'A study of job characteristics as based on the Position Analysis Questionnaire (PAQ)', *Journal of Applied Psychology*, 56, 347–368.

Machin, S. (1995) 'Changes in the relative demand for skills in the UK labour market', Centre for Economic Performance, discussion paper no. 221, London School of Economics.

McKenna, F.P. (1983) 'Accident proneness: a conceptual analysis', *Accident Analysis and Prevention*, 15, 65–71.

McLoughlin, I. and Clark, J. (1994) *Technological Change at Work*, 2nd edition, Buckingham: Open University Press.

Mann, R.D. (1959) 'A review of the relationship between personality and performance in small groups', *Psychological Bulletin*, 56, 241–270.

Martin, R. and Wall, T. (1989) 'Attentional demand and cost responsibility as stressors in shopfloor jobs', *Academy of Management Journal*, 32, 69–86.

Maslow, A.H. (1965) *Eupsychian Management*, Homewood, IL: Irwin.

Maslow, A.H. (1970) *Motivation and Personality*, 2nd edition, New York: Harper & Row.

Matteson, M.T. and Ivancevich, J.M. (1987) *Controlling Work Stress: Effective Human Resource and Management Strategies*, San Francisco: Jossey-Bass.

Mearns, K. and Flin, R. (1996) 'Risk perception in hazardous industries', *The Psychologist*, 9, 401–404.

Messinger, G.S. (1985) *Manchester in the Victorian Age*, Manchester: Manchester University Press.

Miller, R.B. (1962) 'Task description and analysis', in R. Gagne (ed.) *Psychological Principles in System Design*, New York: Holt, Rinehart and Winston.

Miner, J.B. (1983) 'The unpaved road from theory: over the mountains to application', in R.H. Kilmann, K.W. Thomas, D.P. Slevin, R. Nath and S.L. Jerrell (eds) *Producing Useful Knowledge for Organizations*, New York: Praeger.

Morse, N.C. and Reimer, E. (1956) 'The experimental change of a major organizational variable', *Journal of Abnormal Social Psychology*, 51, 120–129.

Muchinsky, P.M. and Tuttle, M.L. (1979) 'Employee turnover: an empirical and methodological assessment', *Journal of Vocational Behavior*, 14, 43–77.

Mullen, B. and Copper, C. (1994) 'The relation between group cohesiveness and performance: an integration', *Psychological Bulletin*, 115, 210–227.

Murphy, L. (1988) 'Workplace interventions for stress reduction and prevention', in C.L. Cooper and R. Payne (eds) *Causes, Coping and Consequences of Stress at Work*, New York: Wiley.

Norman, D. (1988) *The Psychology of Everyday Things*, New York: Basic Books.

O'Driscoll, M. and Cooper, C. (1996) 'Sources and management of excessive job stress and burnout', in P. Warr (ed,) *Psychology at Work*, London: Penguin.

Office of Technology Assessment (1984) *Computerized Manufacturing Automation*, Washington, DC: Government Printing Office.

Olson, J., Card, S., Landauer, T., Olson, G., Malone, T. and Leggett, J. (1993) 'Computer-supported co-operative work: research issues for the 90s', *Behaviour and Information Technology*, 12, 115–129.

Osborn, A.F. (1957) *Applied Imagination*, New York: Charles Scribner's Sons.

Parker, S. and Wall, T. (1996) 'Job design and modern manufacturing', in P. Warr (ed.) *Psychology at Work*, London: Penguin.

Parker, S., Chmiel, N. and Wall, T. (1997) 'Work characteristics and employee well-being within a context of strategic downsizing', *Journal of Occupational Health Psychology*, 2, 289–303.

Patrick, J. (1992) *Training: Research and Practice*, London: Academic Press.

Perrow, C. (1984) *Normal Accidents: Living with High Risk Systems*, New York: Basic Books.

Perrow, C. (1994) 'Accidents in high-risk systems', *Technology Studies Offprint*, 1, 1–20.

Petty, M.M., McGee, G.W. and Cavender, J.W. (1984) 'A meta-analysis of the relationships between individual job satisfaction and individual performance', *Academy of Management Review*, 9, 712–721.

Pidgeon, N., Hood, C., Jones, D., Turner, B. and Gibson, R. (1992) *Risk: Analysis, Perception and Management*, London: The Royal Society.

Pierce, J. and Newstrom, J. (1983) 'The design of flexible work schedules and employee responses: relationships and processes', *Journal of Occupational Behaviour*, 4, 247–262.

Poulton, E.C. (1970) *Environment and Human Efficiency*, Springfield, IL: Charles C. Thomas.

Ramsey, J. and Morrisey, S. (1978) 'Isodecrement curves for task performance in hot environments', *Applied Ergonomics*, 9, 66–72.

Rasmussen, J. (1986) *Human Information Processing and Human Machine Interaction*, Amsterdam: North-Holland.

Reason, J.T. (1974) *Man in Motion*, London: Weidenfeld and Nicolson.

Reason, J.T. (1988) 'Stress and cognitive failure', in S. Fisher and J. Reason (eds) *Handbook of Life Stress, Cognition and Health*, Chichester: Wiley.

Reason, J.T. (1990) *Human Error*, Cambridge: Cambridge University Press.

Reason, J.T. and Mycielska, K. (1982) *Absent-Minded? The Psychology of Mental Lapses and Everyday Errors*, Englewood Cliffs, NJ: Prentice-Hall.

Rissler, A. and Jacobson, L. (1987) 'Cognitive efficiency during high workload in final system testing of a large computer system', in M.J. Bullinger and B. Shackel (eds) *Human Computer Interaction (Interact '87)*, Amsterdam: Elsevier North-Holland.

Robertson, I.T. and Downs, S. (1979) 'Learning and the prediction of performance: development of trainability testing in the United Kingdom', *Journal of Applied Psychology*, 64, 42–50.

Robson, C. (1993) *Real World Research*, Oxford: Blackwell.

Rodrigues, C.A. (1988) 'Identifying the right leader for the right situation', *Personnel*, September, 43–46.

Rogelberg, S., Barnes-Farrell, J. and Lowe, C. (1992) 'The step-ladder technique: an alternative group structure facilitating effective group decision-making', *Journal of Applied Psychology*, 77, 730–737.

Rosenstock, I. (1974) 'The health belief model and preventative health behaviour', *Health Education Monologue*, 2, 356–386.

Rotter, J. (1966) 'Generalised expectancies for internal versus external locus of control', *Psychological Monographs*, 80, whole no. 609.

Sanders, M.S. and McCormick, E.J. (1987) *Human Factors in Engineering and Design*, 6th edition, New York: McGraw-Hill.

Schmitt, N. (1976) 'Social and situational determinants of interview decisions: implications for the employment interview', *Personnel Psychology*, 29, 79–101.

Schneider, J. and Locke, E.A. (1971) 'A critique of Herzberg's incident classification system and a suggested revision', *Organizational Behaviour and Human Performance*, 6, 441–457.

Selye, H. (1936) 'A syndrome produced by diverse noxious agents', *Nature*, 138, 32.

Selye, H. (1976) *The Stress of Life*, 2nd edition, New York: McGraw-Hill.

Senior, B. (1997) 'Team roles and team performance: is there really a link?', *Journal of Occupational and Organisational Psychology*, 70, 241–258.

Sepella, P., Tuominen, E. and Koskinen, P. (1987) 'Job structure and work content in a flexible manufacturing system', in P. Brodner (ed.) *Skill Based Automated Manufacturing*, Oxford: Pergamon.

Shepherd, A. (1996) 'Task analysis as a framework for examining HCI tasks', in A. Monk and G.N. Gilbert (eds) *Perspectives on HCI*, London: Academic Press.

Sinclair, M. (1986) 'Ergonomic aspects of the automated factory', *Ergonomics*, 29, 1507–1523.

Slovic, P., Fischhoff, B. and Lichtenstein, S. (1980) 'Facts and fears: understanding perceived risk', in: R. C. Schwing and W. A. Albers (eds) *Societal Risk Assessment: How Safe Is Safe Enough?*, New York: Plenum Press.

Smallwood, J. (1994) 'Informal knowledge in the safety context', Unpublished MSc thesis, University of Sheffield.

Smith, A. (1995) 'Determinants of human performance in organizational settings', in C. Cooper and I. Robertson (eds) *International Review of Industrial and Organisational Psychology*, vol. 10, London: Wiley.

Sperandio, A. (1978) 'The regulation of working methods as a function of workload among air traffic controllers', *Ergonomics*, 21, 367–390.

Stammers, R. (1996) 'Training and the acquisition of knowledge and skill', in P. Warr (ed.) *Psychology at Work*, London: Penguin.

Steers, R.M. and Porter, L.W. (eds) (1983) *Motivation and Work Behavior*, 3rd edition, New York: McGraw-Hill.

Steiner, I. (1972) *Group Process and Productivity*, Orlando, FL: Academic Press.

Stevens, M. and Campion, M. (1994) 'The knowledge, skill, and ability requirements for teamwork: implications for human resource management', *Journal of Management*, 20, 503–530.

Stogdill, R.M. (1965) *Managers, Employees, Organizations*, Columbus, OH: Ohio State University, Bureau of Business Research.

Strube, M.J. and Garcia, J.E. (1981) 'A meta-analytic investigation of Fiedler's contingency model of leader effectiveness', *Psychological Bulletin*, 90, 307–321.

Suchman, L. (1987) *Plans and Situated Actions*, Cambridge: Cambridge University Press.

Suchman, L. (1993) 'Technologies and accountability: of lizards and aeroplanes', in G. Button (ed.) *Technology in Working Order*, London: Routledge.

Svenson, O. (1989) 'On expert judgements in safety analyses in the process industries', *Reliability Engineering and System Safety*, 25, 219–256.

Swain, A. and Weston, L. (1988) 'An approach to the diagnosis and misdiagnosis of abnormal conditions in post-accident sequences in complex man–machine systems', in L. Goodstein, H. Andersen and S. Olsen (eds) *Tasks, Errors and Mental Models*, London: Taylor and Francis.

Trist, E. and Bamforth, K. (1951) 'Some social and psychological consequences of the longwall method of coal-getting', *Human Relations*, 4, 3–38.

Tuckman, B. (1965) 'Developmental sequences in small groups', *Psychological Bulletin*, 62, 384–399.

Vroom, V.H. (1964) *Work and Motivation*, New York: Wiley.

Waldman, D.A. and Avolio, B.J. (1986) 'A meta-analysis of age differences in job performance', *Journal of Applied Psychology*, 71, 33–38.

Wall, T. and Clegg, C. (1981) 'A longitudinal study of work group design', *Journal of Occupational Behaviour*, 2, 31–49.

Wall, T., Corbett, J., Martin, R., Clegg, C. and Jackson, P. (1991) 'Advanced manufacturing technology, work design, and performance: a change study', *Journal of Applied Psychology*, 75, 691–697.

Wall, T., Jackson, P. and Davids, K. (1992) 'Operator work design and robotics system behaviour: a serendipitous field study', *Journal of Applied Psychology*, 77, 353–362.

Warr, P. (1987) *Work, Unemployment, and Mental Health*, Oxford: Oxford University Press.

Warr, P. (1996) 'Employee well-being', in P. Warr (ed.) *Psychology at Work*, London: Penguin.

Weiman, C. (1977) 'A study of occupational stressors and the incidence of disease risk', *Journal of Occupational Medicine*, 19, 119–122.

Weldon, E. and Weingart, L. (1994) 'Group goals and group performance', *British Journal of Social Psychology*, 32, 307–334.

West, M. (1994) *Effective Teamwork*, Leicester: British Psychological Society.

West, M. (1996) 'Working in groups', in P. Warr (ed.) *Psychology at Work*, London: Penguin.

West, M. and Anderson, N. (1993) 'Innovation, cultural values and the management of change in British hospitals', *Work and Stress*, 6, 293–310.

Wickens, C.D. (1992) *Engineering Psychology and Human Performance*, 2nd edition, New York: HarperCollins.

Wilkinson, R. (1962) 'Muscle tension during mental work under sleep deprivation', *Journal of Experimental Psychology*, 64, 565–571.

Williams, H., Lubin, A. and Goodnow, J. (1959) 'Impaired performance with acute sleep loss', *Psychological Monographs*, 73, 1–26.

Williamson, A. and Feyer, A.-M. (1995) 'Causes of accidents and time of day', *Work and Stress*, 9, 158–164.

Woods, D. (1984) 'Some results on operator performance in emergency events', *Institute of Chemical Engineers Symposium Series*, 90, 21–31.

Wuebker, L. (1986) 'Safety locus of control as a predictor of industrial accident and injuries', *Journal of Business and Psychology*, 1, 19–30.

Zohar, D. (1980) 'Safety climate in industrial organizations: theoretical and applied implications', *Journal of Applied Psychology*, 65, 96–102.

Index

ability tests 51
accident reporting systems
      93
accidents at work 93–4
accidents, error and stress
      98–9
accident-proneness 103
acclimatisation 78
Adams, J. 62
advanced manufacturing
      technology (AMT)
      16, 17, 18, 19, 22,
      24
Allport, D., Antonis, B. and
      Reynolds, P.
      72
AMT *see* advanced
      manufacturing
      technology
Anderson, J. 41, 43
Anderson, N. 50, 51, 129

Annett, J. 30, 31
antecedent behaviour 93
appraisal methods 55–6
assessment centre 53
attitudes to safety 102
Avolio, B. 55

Bamforth, K. 116
Bandura, A. 45
Banks, M. 26
Barrett, G. 53
Bartlett, F. 81, 95
Bass, B. 126
Beehr, T. 36
Beland, F. 109
Belbin, R. 128
Benne, K. 128
Berry, D. 48
Bhagat, R. 36
Blanz, F. 56
Braverman, H. 114

Broadbent, D. 48, 70, 72, 79, 81, 88
Brown, I. 93
burnout 35
Butler, M. 108

Campbell, S. 86
Campion, J. 52
Campion, M. 130, 131, 132
Campion, M., Medsker, G. and Higgs, A. 130, 131
Card, S. 117
case studies 11
Caspar, P. 69
changes in performance with time of day 84–5
Charuwatee, P. 102
Cherns, A. 116
Chi, M., Glaser, R. and Farr, M. 41
Chmiel, N. 48, 74, 81, 89
Chmiel, N., Totterdell, P. and Folkard, S. 74, 81
circadian rhythms 84
Clark, J. 4, 5
Clegg, C. 19, 22, 23, 33, 47
cognitive failures 99, 103
cognitive heuristics 102
cognitive skill acquisition 63, 136
compensatory effort 87
computer supported co-operative work 117–18, 137
contexts for research knowledge 12
Cook, M. 50, 52
Cooper, C. 34, 35
Cooper, C., Cooper, R. and Eaker, L. 35
Cooper, R. 74, 80

Copper, C. 129
Corbett, J. 19, 47
Cordes, C. 35
correlational studies 11
Cox, S. 102
Cox, T. 102
Craig, A. 74, 80
critical incidents technique 26
Crossman, E. 41

Davis, L., Canter, R. and Hoffman, J. 20
Dean, J. 17
declarative knowledge 42
Dedobbeleer, N. 109
Dejoy, D. 102
Diehl, M. 123
disasters 104
distributed cognition 119–22, 137
Dougherty, T. 35
Downs, S. 53
Drucker, P. 56
Duncan, K. 30, 31

Edwards, J. 37
Elkin, A. 33
Ellis, J. 121
employee assistance programmes 38
employment testing 51
ergonomics 66
error reduction 111
error tolerant systems 110–11
Ettlie, J. 19
extrinsic job satisfaction 32

Fanger, P. 78
Farr, J. 55
Farr, M. 41
fatigue 80–1

Ferris, G. 61
Feyer, A.-M. 98
Fiedler, F. 126
field experimentation 10
Fine, B. 77
Fitts, P. 42
Flin, R. 100
Foley, P., Watts, D. and
    Wilson, B. 4, 5
Folkard, S. 85, 86
Folkman, S. 36
Frankenhaeuser, M. 87
French, J., Caplan, R. and
    Harrison, V. 34
Frese, M. 42, 111
Fried, Y. 61
Friedman, M. 36
function allocation 89, 90
functional job analysis 25

Garcia, J. 127
Gardner, G. 101
Gardner, P., Chmiel, N. and
    Wall, T. 48
general health questionnaire 34
George, J. 125
Ghiselli, E. 56
Goldberg, A., Dar-El, E. and
    Rubin, A. 101
Gould, L. 101
Green, C. 101
Greenberg, J. 62
group: cohesiveness 128, 129;
    composition 128;
    development 123;
    effectiveness 129
groups and decision-making
    123–4
groupthink 124
group-working 114
Guzzo, R. 125

Hackman, J. 21, 33, 61, 116
Hamilton, P., Hockey, G.R.
    and Rejman, M. 79
Hancock, P. 89
hawthorne effect 7, 77
Haynes, R.S., Pine, R.C. and
    Fitch, H.G. 107
Herrick, N. 37
Herzberg, F. 60
Hick, W. 72
hierarchical task analysis
    30–1
Higgs, A. 130
Hockey, G. 71, 76, 78, 79, 82,
    86, 87, 88
Holding, D. 81, 88
Holloway, W. 6
human error 95–8, 136
human factors 66–8
human reliability studies 109
Hutchins, E. 118, 119
Hyman, R. 72

Iaffaldano, M. 33
implicit learning 48
individual states and mental
    performance 80–4
information processing approach
    68
intrinsic job satisfaction 32
Ivancevich, J. 37

Jackson, S.E., Schwab, R.L. and
    Schuler, R.S. 35
Jacobson, L. 88
Jaikamur, R. 19
job: analysis 22, 135;
    characteristics model 21,
    61; design 18–22, 135;
    enlargement 20; interview
    50; redesign and

performance 22–4;
rotation 20; sampling 52;
satisfaction 21, 135;
satisfaction and well-being
31–3; simplification 19
job-related stress 33–8
Johansen, R. 117
Jones, A. 108
Jones, J. 103
just in time (JIT) 17, 24

Kahneman, D. 70, 102
Kahneman, D., Slovic, P. and
Tversky, A. 102
Kantowitz, B. 69
Karasek, R. 21, 35
Kelly, J. 19, 22
Kerr, W. 78
Kobrick, J. 77

Landauer, T. 117
Landy, F. 50, 55
lapses 96, 97, 98
latent performance deficits 86–8
Latham, G., Steele, T. and
Saari, L. 45
Lazarus, R. 36
leadership and group-working
125–7
Leggett, J. 117
Locke, E. 60
Lundberg, U. 87

McClelland, D. 59, 60
Maccoby, M. 37
McConkey, D. 56
McCormick, E. 25, 67
McCormick, E.J., Jeanneret, P.R.
and Mecham, R.C. 25
Machin, S. 5
McKenna, F. 103

McLoughlin, I. 4, 5
Malone, T. 117
management by objectives
(MBO) 56–8
Mann, R. 126
Martin, R. 23, 24, 47
Maslow, A. 58, 59
Matterson, M. 37
Mearns, K. 100
Medsker, G. 130
mental capacity 70–2
mental work and technology
68–73
mental workload 69, 70, 136
Messinger, G. 2
Miller, R. 29
Miner, J. 61
mistakes 96, 97, 98
Monk, T. 85
Morrisey, S. 77
Morse, N. 126
motivation at work 58–63
Muchinsky, P. 33
Mullen, B. 129
Murphy, L. 37
Mycielska, K. 99

Newstrom, J. 21
Norman, D. 96, 111

O'Driscoll, M. 34, 35
occupational psychology in the
UK 8
Oldham, G. 21, 33, 61, 116
Olson, J., Card, S., Landauer,
T., Olson, G., Malone, T.
and Leggett, J. 117, 118
Ornstein, S. 62
Osborn, A. 123

Parker, S. 20, 23, 38

Parker, S., Chmiel, N. and
    Wall, T. 38
Patrick, J. 41, 46
performance appraisal 54–8
Perrow, C. 110–11
person–environment (P–E) fit
    34
personnel selection 48–54
Petty, M., McGee, G. and
    Cavender, J. 33
physiological measures 34,
    75
Pidgeon, N. 100, 101
Pidgeon, N., Hood, C., Jones,
    D., Turner, B. and
    Gibson, R. 100
Pierce, J. 21
Porter, L. 58
position analysis questionnaire
    25
post-lunch dip 83, 84, 85
Poulton, E. 78
primary task 74
procedural knowledge 42
psychology and work 6

quality circles 127
quality of work life 37

Ramsey, J. 77
Rasmussen, J. 73, 97
Reason, J. 96, 97, 98, 99, 103,
    104, 107, 110
Reimer, E. 126
response variability 81
risk perception 100–2
risky shift 124
Rissler, A. 88
Robertson, I. 53
Robson, C. 9
Rodrigues, C. 127

Rogelberg, S., Barnes-Farrell, J.
    and Lowe, C. 124
Rogers, Y. 121
Rosch, P. 33
Rosenmann, R. 36
Rosenstock, I. 100
Rotter, J. 103

safety climate 108–9
safety programmes 107–8
Sanders, M. 67
Scallen, F. 89
Schmitt, N. 50
Schneider, J. 60
scientific management 6, 7, 19,
    20, 24, 28, 114
secondary task 74
selection tests 49
Selye, H. 34
Senior, B. 128
Sepella, P., Tuominen, E. and
    Koskinen, P. 19
Shackleton, V. 50, 51
Shea, G. 125
Sheats, P. 128
Shepherd, A. 28
shiftwork 85–6
Sinclair, M. 19
single channel information
    processor 72
skill acquisition 40–3
skilled performance 43
sleep loss 82
slips 94, 96, 97, 98
Slovic, P., Fischhoff, B. and
    Lichtenstein, S. 101
Smallwood, J. 102
Smith, A. 80, 83, 84, 85
Smith, Adam 19
Snell, S. 17
social loafing 125

socio-technical systems 115–17, 137
Sperandio, A. 87
Stammers, R. 45
Steers, R. 58
Steiner, I. 125
Stevens, M. 131, 132
Stogdill, R. 126
stress management 37
Stroebe, W. 123
Strube, M. 127
subjective workload measures 75
Suchman, L. 118, 119
supervisory control 88
superworkers 42
Svenson, O. 102
Swain, A. 110

task activity 73
task allocation 88–90
task analysis 27–30, 45, 135
Tattersall, A. 76
Taylor, F. 7, 19
team viability 129
team-working and performance 124–5
technology at work 3
Three Mile Island 104, 106
total quality management (TQM) 17
trainability tests 53
training 45; evaluation 46; needs 44; programmes 44; for technology in the future 46–8
Trist, E. 116
Tuckman, B. 123
Tuttle, M. 33

type A personalities 36

verbal protocols 97
violations 96, 100, 137
Vroom, V. 62

Waldman, D. 55
Wall, T. 20, 22, 23, 24, 47, 48, 89
Wall, T., Corbett, J., Martin, R., Clegg, C. and Jackson, P. 23, 47
Wall, T., Jackson, P. and Davids, K. 47
Warr, P. 32
Watts, D. 4
Weiman, C. 36
Weingart, L. 124, 125
Weldon, E. 124, 125
West, M. 115, 124, 129
Weston, L. 110
Wickens, C. 71, 75, 93, 110
Wilkinson, R. 86
Williams, H., Lubin, A. and Goodnow, J. 82
Williamson, A. 98
Wilson, B. 4
Woods, D. 98
work environment and performance 76–80
work groups 127–32
workload measures 73–6
workplace industrial relations survey (WIRS) 4, 5
Wuebker, L. 103

Zapf, D. 42
Zohar, D. 108, 109